Life From a Sitting-Down Perspective

Jessica Pabst

Order this book online at www.trafford.com
or email orders@trafford.com

Most Trafford titles are also available at major online book retailers.

Printed in the United States of America.

ISBN: 978-1-4669-9564-2 (sc)
ISBN: 978-1-4669-9563-5 (e)

Trafford rev. 09/13/2013

www.trafford.com

North America & international
toll-free: 1 888 232 4444 (USA & Canada)
phone: 250 383 6864 ♦ fax: 812 355 4082

I know a place with no

Anger or fears,

As well as a place with no

Sadness or tears

I truly hope with this book

I have written for you,

You will soon come to know

These same places too

"Let me, let me, let me lead the way"

–"I'll take you there" (1)
by
The Staple Singers

Contents

Introduction

Photo by Suzy O'Donnell

My name is Jessie Pabst. Yes, Pabst like the beer. I am not related, but it does make it much easier to give my name out to people on the phone! I have some thoughts and experiences to share. The main experience is a car accident in 2000, when I was sixteen. This left me with paralysis and a traumatic brain injury. I have adjusted to my disabilities and learned many things throughout the last twelve years that I believe could aid other people who have similar disabilities. I know that it would have helped me much to have had an "instruction manual" for paralysis, so I am writing this hoping to help anyone I can. I am aware that not all injuries and paralysis levels are the same as mine, and therefore not all abilities are the same as mine. However, I think the information I have included can help many people in many situations.

I also hope that my words will be able to help people in ways that hospitals cannot. There are of course physical and occupational therapy manuals that have exercises to strengthen the areas that will be used more, and instruct methods of transfers and other basic activities. While the manuals are helpful for those things, there is much more to deal with for which there are no manuals or instruction books. There is much mental and emotional growth needed to come to terms with all new situations, especially paralysis and other disabilities. I have included my tips for all these areas, and I hope they help.

I have written about my belief of living life to its fullest. I have been through much in my life, not all of it positive.   When you come close to death and go through major trials as I have, attitudes and priorities change. I believe in acknowledging and not ignoring the bad, but also that life is too short to dwell on that and be stuck in sadness. It is important to remember that you are stronger than any frustration or sadness, and it is your right to enjoy your life. When you feel the negative feelings coming on, rise above them. Then move on from there and make life positive as possible.

Even if no misfortunes are experienced, it is still important to live the best life possible. I have included some of the things that I believe can help anyone to do that. One of those is to think of all the treasures you have in your life and how lucky you are to have them. I hope to help people see that nothing should bring their world to an end and life is to be enjoyed, sitting or standing!

Quotes from four great men whose messages parallel my own, as you will read:

"A hero is an ordinary individual who finds the strength to persevere and endure in spite of overwhelming obstacles." (2)

– Christopher Reeve, actor and quadriplegic

"Never put off till tomorrow what you can do today." (3)

– Thomas Jefferson

"What would life be if we had no courage to attempt anything?" (4)

– Vincent van Gogh

"The measure of who we are is what we do with what we have." (5)

And

"The difference between a successful person and others is not a lack of strength, not a lack of knowledge, but rather a lack of will." (6)

– Vince Lombardi, former head coach of
my favorite football team the Green Bay Packers

<u>Story</u>
My car accident

January 22, 2000, my friend and I were leaving another friend's house. He lived a little outside our town of Zionsville, located just northwest of Indianapolis. We were in a Toyota Tercel, which is not a very big car. My friend was driving, and the road was icy because it was snowing. We began to slide off the road to the right, and she tried to correct by turning the wheel back to the left. This worked and we got all four wheels back onto the road, but the ice caused us to continue turning even after she straightened the wheel. We did a complete U-turn on the road, so we were then on the other side of the road pointed back out of town.

The driver of a semi was leaving town, and when our car stopped turning we were right in front of him. The speed limit there was 45, and he had no time or space to slow down before hitting us. Due to that, and the car's small size, we felt the full impact of the hit. He ran into the back driver's side of the car, so I was thrown forward and to the left. I hit my head, and then the momentum threw me between the two front bucket seats into the back. This crushed one vertebra of my spine and broke four others.

The vertebrae affected were T5–T9. These are the thoracic vertebrae, which are in the middle section of the spine, so my paralysis level is right above my belly button. My injury is not "complete," which is a severed spinal cord, so I do still have some feeling in my lower half. My lower half is always tingling like a body part does after it has fallen asleep and starts getting blood back. With the incomplete injury I can also feel things like rubbing on my thigh and my toes being touched. This is good because I know if they are ever squished in my shoes or in any other bad position.

When I was thrown forward I also collapsed both of my lungs. When the accident was over and the car finally stopped I was lying in the middle of the back seat with my legs still between the two front seats.

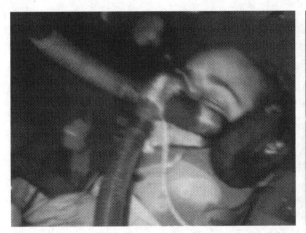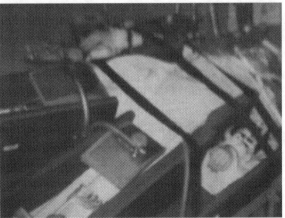

The pictures above show the ventilator and the rotating bed, or "turn table," which helps breathing of patients whose lungs have become filled with fluid by rocking them back and forth gently. This allows the fluid to drain, reducing pressure on the lungs.

Beside paralysis and lung collapse, I hit my head so hard that I was in a coma for one week. The section of my brain that was injured was the left frontal lobe, and one of its main functions is controlling the short-term memory. After I woke up from the coma, I could remember the words to old songs on the radio that my mom brought in, but nothing short-term. I could not even remember that I had been in the accident or that I was paralyzed. My mom told me that I had to be reminded of it daily for some time.

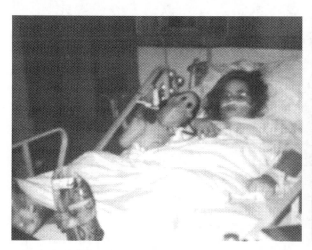 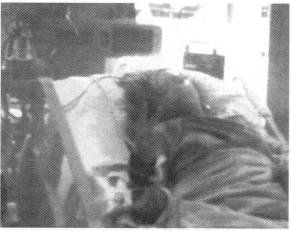

Things were hard but I kept my cool, as can be seen in the pictures. The first picture of me in my hospital bed shows my stuffed animal Opus. I received him as a gift for my sixth birthday after my eye injury (in "Trials" section), and I slept with him every night I was at home, even in my teenage years. He was in my hospital bed with me while I was in a coma, and after I came out of it. In that picture you can also see my plastic foot boots. They kept my feet from dropping at the ankles because that would have greatly atrophied my calf muscle. I wore these almost all the time to keep the muscle stretched. What I liked about them was the coloring that we chose. There were sets with solid colors, but I chose tie-dye because I thought they were awesome!

The second picture is of me in my bed giving the peace sign. I did this to show that even though I had been through much I was still me. My friend told me she was going to take the picture, and that was my automatic reaction. The smile I am giving in that picture is a genuine one, not just a response to someone taking a picture. It helped to reinforce that the accident did not change me.

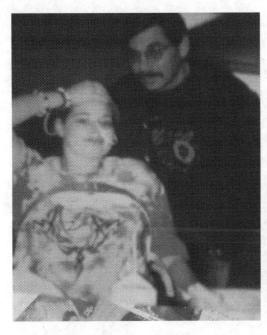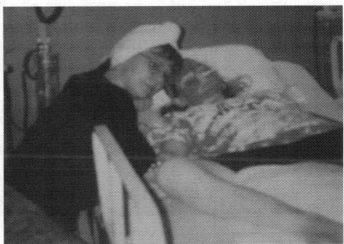

I then had surgery to stabilize my broken spine. This involved cutting in my back but also in my side to get to the spine from a different angle. The first picture above, with my dad, shows the brace that I wore for a period of time after my surgery to keep my spine straight until the bones knitted together and stabilized. The tube coming out of my nose is called an "NG" tube, which stands for "nasogastric." This is used for nutrition because most all spinal cord injury patients lose their appetites for a time after their injury. Nurses would put the nutritional shake through the tube into my stomach a couple times a day to help me get all the calories and vitamins I needed.

The second picture, with my mom, shows that one can find joy despite the difficulties of any situation. Everything does not need to be sad! My mom and I decided that we wanted to pamper ourselves and have a beauty day. This helped me relax after all the activities I had done, but also recharge myself for all the activities I still had to do. Most of all, it made me smile. Also, notice that in both pictures I am wearing my cool tie-dye Grateful Dead shirt!

During my rehabilitation I had a very full schedule. I had physical therapy, occupational therapy, speech therapy and schooling. Much of my physical therapy time was spent on a large mat only a foot off of the ground learning how to do basic movements. The therapists taught me to roll myself over and then push myself up into a sitting position. Once I had learned that, they taught me about finding my center of gravity so I could balance and not fall back over and hurt myself. From there I learned how to manually move my legs so I did not injure them.

This was very difficult, and I remember thinking many times how much easier things probably would have been if my legs were not there. I do still think that sometimes, but then I remind myself of the possibility of walking again with the power of technology.

The first promising study is that of stem cells. These are cells that are able become many different cell types, including spinal cord, and then self renew to create more of the same cells. This is encouraging for many different areas, but especially for spinal cord injury patients. My basic understanding of this is the doctors could implant the stem cells into my spinal cord, and those cells would mimic the spinal cord cells all around them. In doing this they would fill in any gaps of my cord and I would be able to move the muscles I could not before.

As I said, this technology is still being studied and tested. I am sure it will take some time before it is able to be used on people, and once it is open to the public I'm sure it will be very expensive. Until the day when everyone is able to be helped with this for low prices, we must not get ahead of ourselves.

There is a study that does involve removal of limbs: Bionics. This is the replacement or enhancement of organs or other body parts with mechanical versions. They are better than just prostheses in that they mimic the original function very closely, or even surpass it. The study of this technology is also in a very early stage, but judging by the speed of past technological developments hopefully this will not take very long. Scientists have said that users of the mechanical body parts may even be able to move the limbs by thought alone, i.e. the person thinks that they want to move the leg and the sensors pick that thought up and move the leg. This is an example of technology blowing my mind, but I am very thankful for it!

In the hospital, the "PT's" (Physical therapists) also taught me ways to strengthen my upper half so that I was able to do all the actions. The important thing is that they taught me to do them without pulling any muscles. When your lower half doesn't work, the last thing you want to do is injure the upper half. I safely strengthened by lifting weights and using a Thera-band (in "Para-tips" section).

The "OT's" (Occupational therapists) taught me how to do everyday activities with paralysis. I learned to dress my lower half, which involved putting on underwear and pants one leg at a time, lying back flat on the bed and rolling side to side while pulling up the clothing of the side that I was not putting weight on at the time.

We also worked on bathroom activities. They taught me the best ways to shower in a chair now that I was paralyzed. Finding my center of gravity while doing this was much harder. It is extremely difficult to hold balance while shampooing hair with both hands and eyes closed. The other difficulty in the shower is the 'slippery factor.' You have to be very careful when washing legs and feet because you don't want to injure a leg by dropping it. I always make sure that my shower chair has enough "dump" (as I explain in "My Chair" section) that I feel comfortable. This allows me to wash more freely because I am not afraid I will fall out of the chair.

The OT's helped me to realize that paralysis was not the end of the world for me and that I could still do most of the things I could before, now just with a little more effort. They also regularly reminded me that all of these tasks would become easier and take less time as I did them more regularly, and over time I have realized this is true. As with all new things, practice makes perfect (or in this case, practice makes better and faster).

Occupational therapy also helped me with writing. When I first tried to write after the accident, my handwriting was very small and downhill because the brain injury also affected that area of my brain. My mom told me it was almost microscopic. The therapists had me practice handwriting for many sessions: holding the pen correctly, making my letters larger and staying between the lines (just like when I learned as a kid). In all, physical and occupational therapies both worked on the redevelopment of my motor skills.

Speech therapy helped me recover as much as I could from my brain injury. In this therapy we did brain puzzles and memory exercises. The puzzles, such as crosswords, were to help revive and use my brain muscle after being in a coma. The first sessions used exercises to test my capacity and recollection power to see where I was having difficulties. From there the sessions mainly focused on helping the area in which I was lacking, short-term memory. The therapists helped me exercise that area of my brain so it would become stronger, but also helped me develop methods of working around the injury. An example of this is the "TB, BF" letter method I use in the pillow tip that you will see in the helpers section.

There was a full-time teacher on the rehabilitation floor who helped me keep up with my studies. I was in tenth grade at the time of my accident, so I had to do enough schoolwork that I would not fall behind. I remember saying to her, half-comically, "Man, I don't get to stop doing schoolwork even if I've been hit by a truck? No fair!" I did not like having to do the schoolwork along with everything else and felt very overloaded the majority of the time I was in the hospital.

All the activities did however keep me busy enough that I did not have time to sit around and feel sorry for myself, which is what I believe I would have done if I had just stayed in my bed all day long. The therapists were all business and helped me learn how to deal with and adapt to the changes. Though I did not like that at the time, I am thankful for it now. I was released after a little more than three months, on April 28, and allowed to go home. After my release my mom stayed home to help me and I continued doing all that the therapists taught me. With time, I adjusted to life in a chair.

After I was released, I went back to school. The brain injury did make classes and remembering the new things I was learning difficult, but not impossible. I finished high school and moved on to college at IUPUI (Indiana University Purdue University Indianapolis). I graduated with a degree in Spanish Education after 5 years. Again, this was difficult but not impossible.

I have since decided that a profession teaching Spanish would be too difficult. I don't think that my memory would be efficient enough to work with a large number of students, i.e. What Jennifer Smith in my third period Spanish 2 class asked me on the Tuesday before last. That would be hard for anyone, but impossible for me. I do know I would like to work with the language in my career and I plan to translate this book into Spanish, as well as other languages, to help as many people as I can.

The car accident was not the first misfortune to happen to me, as you will read. When people learn about the things that have happened to me and all I have been through they are amazed that I am still here, and even more that I am still happy. I then tell them my outlook on life:

I have two choices of what to do. I can stay inside and cry, or get out and live my life. I have been, and still am, sad at times. When I get the sad feelings I deal with them because I know it is important to not ignore or bury them. Then I rise above and move on. Crying will not reverse what happened to make me sad, so there is no point. I believe all crying will do is make me have to buy more tissues and give me wrinkles! My ultimate view:

<u>It is much better to live With a smile on your Face than tears!</u>

Trials
Tests of Life

Something that always helps me when I have bad times is comedy. I like comedic movies and television, but I also like to do my own. I believe that when things make you sad it is possible to make them positive so that you are not sad every time you think about them. One day I decided to do that with my bad times:

My misfortunes, as an ice-cream sundae

Bowl: Birth and Infancy

My mother had hyperemesis gravidarum (a severe form of morning sickness) when she was pregnant with me, and was admitted to the hospital ten times during her pregnancy. I was born on the tenth visit after an amniocentesis showed my lungs were developed. I was one month premature and weighed five pounds and four ounces. My mom told me that she used to think of me as "her little package." I did not have to go to the premature nursery, but I was the smallest baby in the regular one. Even though I was premature and very small, I was able to go home after only three days.

Spoon: Eye Injury

When I was born, I was slightly cross-eyed. The doctor does not fix this until a child is around five years old. My doctor did that for me at that age and my vision was fine. Then, not even a year later, I had an accident:

We were getting ready for a party for my birthday, which is in June. We were having the party outside because it was so warm and sunny. I was opening a plastic package of picnic table cloths, and I pulled up too forcefully with the scissors. This not only made the blade of the scissors go through the plastic, but also reverse back towards my face. The point of the blade pierced the surface of my eye and the lens in the middle of my eye.

We of course had to cancel the party and call my eye doctor. It was just before his closing time of noon on a Saturday. We went to his office and had him look at it. Luckily I did not pierce my brain, but I was only about an inch from doing so. After examining my eye he tracked down the best eye surgeon he knew and told him what happened.

I don't care about my eye injury because I got Ken,
Barbie and their hot dog stand!

We met with him and the broken lens was removed, but due to my age he was not able to put a new lens in until my eye was fully grown when I was fifteen years old. Due to this, my vision was 20/1600 in that eye from age six to fifteen. This means that if someone with perfect vision could see something from sixteen hundred feet away, I would have to be twenty feet away to see the same thing clearly.

After I had the lens implant surgery at age fifteen, my eye was extremely delicate and I had to be very careful in all of my activities. It was fine for a couple days, but then I accidentally hit my head and detached the retina in that eye. It was similar to a black curtain being dropped over the eye. I was out of town on vacation when I did this, so I was not able to go to my doctor's office until I returned home. When I did see him he decided that I needed emergency surgery to repair the injury. I had that surgery successfully, and now the vision in that eye is even better than in my right. Now I am **very** careful and protective of my eyes!

Ice Cream: Car Accident

I suffered broken back bones, paralysis and both of my lungs were collapsed. It was also much more complicated for me to get out and do anything than it had been before, so I lost many of my friends.

Whipped Cream: Traumatic Brain Injury

As I said, I also suffered one of these in the car accident. I was in a coma for a week, had to learn how to do many things again and it does still somewhat affect my short-term memory.

Chocolate Sauce: Spasms

I suffered from these severely and had to take a fair amount of oral anti-spasm medication to quiet them before I had my Medtronic Baclofen Pump (in "Tips" section) implanted. The level of medication I needed made me sleep between fifteen and twenty hours a day when I was taking it in pill form. The pump changed that. It is an electronic device implanted in the abdomen that continually delivers medicine to the body based on settings that can be adjusted by computer. The best part about the pump is that the medicine is delivered by way of a tube that is connected directly to the spinal cord. Now the Baclofen does not need to go through my brain at all, so it leaves me clear-headed.

However, there are plus-sides to the spasms. The first is when I put weight on my legs after I haven't for a while they will spasm, continually bouncing until my feet are comfortable on the foot plate. I used to think this was bad, and I would try to make it stop by forcing the foot down on the footplate. I have since realized there is nothing wrong with the bouncing as long as it does eventually stop (about 15-20 seconds). Now when they start jumping, I remember that is using leg muscles, so it is actually helping me.

The other plus to the spasms is that they occur when something on my lower half is irritated. This way, I know if something is uncomfortable or there is pain in my legs and/or my toes. They help me to not injure myself (example: My legs will jump if something on my lap is hurting my thighs).

Caramel: Pain

I was in a lot of pain, so I had the hardware in my back replaced one year after my accident. I do still have pain from everyday activity, but I have learned ways to reduce pain which I have shared in my tips section.

Butterscotch: Engagement

I was engaged, but my fiancé decided he wanted live in Florida. My entire family is here in Indiana and I knew that I could not leave them or my house, so we decided not to get married. It is sad, but I wish him nothing but the best.

Chocolate Chips: Dad

My father recently passed away. He had fought stomach and liver problems for a while, and they ultimately took him away from us. I miss him very much, but I know he is still with me. As you read on, you will see the signs he has given to assure me of this.

Chopped Peanuts: Kitties

I had a cat that I loved very much. I named her Ali so I could call her my Ali cat ('alley cat,' haha). She was the best pet I had ever had. She loved me very much. She loved attention, but also left me alone when I wanted.

She was very easy to please: her favorite toys to play with were milk rings. She would push them around on the hard floors and then chase them so she could push them again. She would also push them under the foot plate of my standing frame (in "Tips") and try to get them back out. If I did not see any on the floor, I knew I would be able to find some there.

She loved to talk to me and would all the time. The meows were not just in one manner. There were the multi-syllable (moww-wow) ones, and even ones in different tones (moww? Or moww!). I had her for more than four years. One weekend when I was not at home, my roommate called and told me he had found her passed away. I am sad about it, but instead of concentrating on that I choose to think about all the good times I had with her.

After I had my closure with her passing, I went to the animal shelter to look for a new cat. I always go to the shelter to look for animals because there are so many great pets there that need homes. When I saw this cat, I knew he was for me. I hadn't had a boy pet since my ferret when I was in my early teen years. The name that the shelter had given him was Hutch.

What I loved about Hutch was how relaxed he was all the time. He was my little sweetie! He never jumped or ran around, and never attacked me (even playing) as some cats do. After I had him for a couple months, he began acting strange. He would not eat anything, and he was behaving as if his stomach was hurting him. I took him to my vet's office, where they did an ultrasound and told me that there was a lump inside his intestines.

The doctor said that in order to find out if it was cancer they would have to do a very expensive surgery that he may not survive, and that his blood tests already showed liver failure. He said that in his opinion euthanasia was the most humane decision. It broke my heart, but I did have him put to sleep. It makes me feel better to believe that my dad and my Ali cat are on the other side with him, and that I may see them all again one day.

Sprinkles: Epilepsy

I was recently diagnosed with Epilepsy as a result of my brain injury. While I did not have violent body seizures, I experienced episodes in which I zoned out. My mom told me that when this happened she could be in my face saying my name and waving her hands, and I would only blankly stare ahead as if she was not even there.

I was not allowed to drive for six months because of this and the doctor prescribed two medications, which means I now have eight more pills to take every day (and they are giant!). However, I am no longer having the seizures and am allowed to drive again.

Cherry on top: Fire

I recently had a fire that destroyed my bedroom and whose smoke damaged most of the rest of my house. It destroyed my bookcase headboard that had both my keepsake box and my medical notebook in it. The box had everything that I have loved and treasured enough to keep throughout my whole life. The notebook, as you will see in my "Helpers" section, had all of my medical information from the last two years in it.

What I lost in the fire which hurt me the most, beside the box, was my stuffed penguin Opus that you just read about in my "Story" section. I had slept with him almost every night since I got him, which was around twenty years before.

Luckily I did have insurance, so my house was restored. Everything that I lost does still hurt, but I do not dwell on that because that will not bring them back and it will only make me upset.

Milk to go with the sundae: Upper Body

Not being able to use my legs, I now do **everything** with my arms. Over time, this is starting to cause problems. My shoulders have been hurting a lot lately. I will continue doing stretches for this and work with a physical therapist if I feel I should.

Doing everything with my arms has also given me restless arm syndrome. Before the accident I had restless leg syndrome. This happens when you use the limbs all day and then go to bed, where you do not use them at all. The definition of the syndrome states that it is "an irresistible urge to move the limb." I remember thinking one of the benefits of my paralysis would be it going away, but it instead just moved up to my arms!

However, on the positive side, my arms are now **awesome**. I look like a bodybuilder when I flex. People ask me if I work out and if I have any tips for them to get muscles like mine. I say, comically, that I work out all day and all they need to do is use a wheelchair for twelve years. Ha-ha!

My point in saying all of these things is not to upset anyone, or make people pity me. I am trying to show that I am not going to let these things make me sad. I have goals and I am not going to let anything stop me from accomplishing them!

Para-Tips
Things that I have learned over the years that I
Would like to share, and that I hope will help

My shirt says "Tough Times Never Last. Tough People Do."

Helpers

1) Remote Controls (beyond just the television remote)

These are especially convenient for overhead lights and fans. There are also remote starters for cars. This helps to warm the car up in the winter and cool it down in the summer without having to make trips and do transfers to start the car with the key. I love all of mine.

2) Transfer (or "slide") Boards

Transfers are going to and from a wheelchair to another surface (bed, chair, toilet, etc.). These may be difficult in the beginning, but they do become easier and faster over time. An aid that helped me with transfers in the beginning was a "slide-board," a finished wood or plastic board that can be used to bridge the gap between the wheelchair and another surface. I used one until I felt strong and comfortable enough to do my transfers without it. They are flat with sloped ends, and have slots for your hand to maneuver the board into place.

My steps:

1) Lock brakes on chair.

2) Slide board under bottom, with the other end where I want to transfer.

3) Push body off of where I was sitting and about halfway over on the board.

4) Reach to where I am transferring and pull myself over the rest of the way.

5) Practice with supervision until you are comfortable performing them alone:

    – Chair to bed, and the reverse

    – Chair to couch (or other chair, such as a recliner), and the reverse

    – Chair to toilet, and the reverse

    – Chair to shower chair or bench, and the reverse

    – Chair to car, and the reverse (the handle on the inside roof of the car is also helpful for these transfers. Just be careful to not put too much weight on it).

Quick tip: putting a pillowcase over the board can make transfers easier and more comfortable, especially against bare skin.

3) Leg Rolls

    When I'm sitting somewhere with my legs straight out in front of me, I have found that putting small pillows or a rolled blanket under my knees helps keep my legs from experiencing spasms. It also helps to relieve back pain because bending at the knee takes the stress off the spine by maintaining the optimum "pelvic tilt," and that relaxes the lower muscles of the back. These are also helpful if you have something on your lap that you don't want to slide off.

4) <u>Basic Pain Relievers</u>

<u>Ice Pack</u>

Relying on the upper body for all activities causes soreness and stiffness. Ice packs help to take the edge and sharpness off the pain. I have three different packs in my freezer. The version I choose depends on the severity and area size of my pain. If my whole back is in pain I prefer the large thin pad. If there is only one area with sharp pain I use the thicker round version. With this, lying on a flat surface will press it in to the muscle, not just against it. The third is another large flat I keep as a spare to use while the others refreeze.

<u>Heat Pad</u>

After the pain has been reduced with the use of the ice pack, the heat helps to relax the muscle and make the pain go away (Hint: C before H). I only have one version of this: the flat rectangle. Just do not use this for long periods of time or pain could become worse due to increased blood flow.

There are also combination packs available. These can be kept in the freezer to be used as an ice pack, but also warmed in the microwave to be used as a heat pad. With this there is less hassle.

<u>Massage Pad</u>

Another good method of relieving pain is to use a massage pad. The electronic pulsation stimulates the muscles and removes tension. The vibration massages the muscle continuously with no fluctuation for the amount of time it is on. There are even massage pads that also heat up. This is a 2-in-1 for pain relief. I did have one of these, but after my fire I was able to buy a recliner with a built-in massager. I use it daily and like it very much!

<u>Magnetic Pad</u>

It has been found that when held against the skin, magnets relax capillary walls. This boosts blood flow to the painful area and relieves pain. They prevent the muscle spasms, which are the underlying reason for many forms of pain because they interfere with normal contractions and cause discomfort.

Magnets are also able to interfere with the electrochemical reactions within nerve cells. This impedes the cell's ability to transmit the messages of pain to the brain, so the user does not feel it. A positive of the magnet pad, as well as the three previous pads, is that there are no side effects or risk of overdose (compared to medications).

5) Centers For Pain Relief treatments: centersforpainrelief.com [7]

I have not tried any of these, but review them and talk to your doctor if you feel any could help you.

HVLA (Joint manipulation)

HVLA stands for high velocity low amplitude, and refers to a type of joint manipulation. This loosens any chemical buildup between bones that can cause pain. It relieves that pain, while also bringing nutrients from new blood to the tissues in the adjacent bones. It can also relax tight muscles and help with a reflex in parts of the brain for pain relief.

There is much cracking, which can be scary for some people, but it has been shown to help people with both back pain and headaches. It is preformed by doctors and qualified technicians, and there are some risks. Again, talk to your doctor if you feel this could help and would like to try it.

Radio-frequency Ablation or Facet Rhizotomy

In this a needle uses heat to warm the nerve, which interrupts the pain signal to the brain and the spinal cord. It works below the skin and muscle directly to nerves on the bone. It is done using an x-ray machine and usually only takes thirty minutes. The pain relief with this lasts very long: up to a year or more in some patients. It may even relieve pain for life.

The other good thing is that it is usually covered by insurance. The only bad thing is that the pain could get worse before it gets better, but I feel that is worth it and will definitely be looking into it!

Antidepressants

Along with treating depression disorders, researchers have found evidence that tricyclic type of these are effective for the treatment of many different pain conditions. These include migraine headaches and neuropathic pain, which is the sharp and shocking type.

Injections

There are many different choices of these including steroids, toxins, local anesthetics, and opoids:

- Steroids reduce inflammation and pain.

- Toxins cause temporary paralysis.

- Opoid analgesics reduce the number of pain signals sent by the nervous system and the brain's reaction to those. This lessens the perception of pain and calms your response to that pain.

Implantable Devices

A "spinal cord stimulator" or "dorsal column stimulator" is an implantable medical device used to treat chronic pain of neurological origin. It produces electric impulses near the dorsal, or sensory, surface of the spinal cord. This produces a tingling sensation that alters the perception of pain by the patient.

An "Intrathecal Medication Pump" (spinal morphine pump) may be best if high doses of oral pain medications have ceased to relieve pain. This is the same as the Baclophen pump, but instead filled with a pain reliever. It is also possible to have both in the pump at once. Of course there are also risks with this.

In addition to pain relief, the block injections are also used to provide diagnostic information such as helping to determine the pain source.

Gua Sha

This is a healing technique used in Asia that involves rubbing, much like a massage. The skin is pressured by a round-edged tool in strokes. This breaks small capillary blood vessels. The breaking removes any blood stagnation and promotes normal circulation.

Patients experience immediate relief from pain. It does cause the skin to turn red, but that will fade in a couple days. This technique can also help cold symptoms such as fever, cough, chill, nausea, and can be used to prevent and treat upper respiratory and digestive problems.

<u>Kyphoplasty</u>

This is a small spinal surgical procedure that is used to treat vertebral compression fractures. An inflatable bone tamp on the end of a needle is implanted in the vertebra and inflated. This lifts the vertebrae apart and reduces any compression pain that my be felt.

<u>Inexpensive choices</u>

Helichrysum oil-rub on tense muscles to relax and help joint pain.

Herbal Plaster strips-leave on a couple hours. Can use 4-5 a day. Don't use if any skin cuts or bruises.

6) <u>Medications</u>

There are many medications that come with paraplegia, depending on the level and the severity of the injury. I now take an overactive bladder medication every day as well as an antibiotic to prevent any bladder infections. Without these medications, I could become incontinent. I also take two different types of pain pills every day: a painkiller and a muscle relaxer. I also take vitamins every evening. In tip number eleven I have my medication list and explanations.

7) <u>Pill Packs</u>

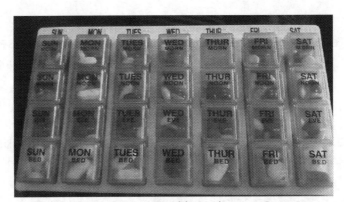

My One Day at a Time Weekly Medication Organizer
Apothecary products Inc

With paralysis comes the need for many pills, as you have just seen. Pill packs are very helpful in pill organization and scheduling. There are many different types available, separated both by days and by times of the day, depending on how many sections are needed. I also keep a small bottle of various pills in the bag on my chair in case I ever need extra while I am away from my house.

8) Journal

The journal is a good method for recording doctor appointments and any other information. In my journal I write the date, what I talked about with my doctor, and then what he or she told me to do. It helps to keep track of anything medical that I think I may need to know in the future. It is also good for writing down feelings, good and bad, and for venting if one of those feelings is anger. It helps to acknowledge any frustrations and get them out.

I write down what is frustrating me and why. Then if I find a solution to that problem I write that also. This gives me something to refer to if I again run across that problem or something similar in the future. You can write these by hand, or on the computer if you prefer (less of a chance of losing it).

9) House Basket

Carrying things around the house can be difficult when you are not able to use your legs. It takes longer, and there is a larger chance of dropping what you have. To help this, I use a basket. It is so great being able to put things in it and go to a different room at a normal speed!

10) The Grabber

This is a device with a handle and a trigger at one end connected to suction cups at the opposite end. It can reach things that I no longer can. I use it in other ways than grabbing things up high, i.e. getting a magazine off the far end of the table. Just be careful trying to pick up heavy or fragile items.

11) Medication List

The list that I created is a table that is divided into columns. The first column has the name of the medication. The next has the dosage in milligrams, or how I take it if it is not a pill. The third column lists when I take the medication and the fourth is the reason for it. Finally, the fifth has the name and number of the doctor that prescribes that for me. This is in case a different doctor has any questions for that doctor.

Jessie Pabst 6/15/1983   Tetanus shot: 8/15/09

Name	Mg	When Taken	For	Doctor&Phone#
Trimethoprim	100	Morning	Bladder	Dr. A, 444-4444
Vesicare	10	Morning	Bladder	Same
Tramadol HCL	50	Morning&afternoon	Pain	Dr. B, 555-5555
Cyclobenzaprine	10	Morning&afternoon	Muscle pain	Same
Levetiracetam	1500	Morning & night	Epilepsy	Dr. C, 666-6666
Vimpat	200	Morning & night	Epilepsy	Same
Magnesium Oxide	400	Night	Epilepsy, muscle pain	Same
Mirapex	0.25	Night	Restless arms	Dr. D
Baclofen	Pump	See paper	Spasms	Dr. E
Fluticasone Propionate	Spray	Night	Congestion	Same

Others

Ibuprofen	400	Morning, afternoon, evening	Headache, overall pain
Peri-colace	200	Afternoon	Bowels
Aspirin	81	Evening	Pain, heart health

Vitamins

     This not only helps when refilling pill packs, but also at doctor's
appointments. Before I made the list, every time I went to any of my doctors'
offices I had to write down all of them individually. This was a hassle, especially
if you have more than one type of doctor, as many people with disabilities do.
Now I can simply give them my list and they make a copy to put in my file. This
is nice for me because it is simple, but also nice for the office because not all
handwriting is easy to read. I have heard many times from office workers and
nurses what a great idea this is.

12) Baclofen Pump

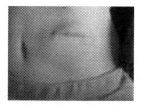

   As I said, a valuable medication for paraplegics with incomplete injuries is a muscle relaxer called Baclofen. Following a spinal cord injury the nerve cells below the level of injury become disconnected from the brain due to scar tissue forming in the damaged area of the spinal cord.

   When the body is stimulated in certain ways, an exaggeration of normal reflexes is sent to the brain through the spinal cord. The brain assesses the stimulant, and if it is thought to not be dangerous the brain sends the signal down to cancel the reflex from moving the muscle. In people with spinal cord injuries, the cancel signal is blocked by the damage in the cord and the reflex is able to continue. This results in a contraction of the muscle.

   These can be very difficult to deal with in some cases. In some people every little thing they do can make the muscle contract and release, resulting in what I call a "jump." Jumping when trying to do anything, especially sleep, is extremely frustrating. Mine got so bad sometimes that I would just lie there crying and asking why it had to be so hard. There are also occasions in which the muscle contracts and will not release, making the leg just stretch out straight. This makes any motions or activities very difficult. Mine prevented me from even being able to have my feet up on the foot plate of my chair.

   To treat this I took more pills. As I said, mine got to the point I was taking so much that I was sleeping 20 hours a day. A little over a year after my accident I talked to my doctor about this, and he told me about the pump. I chose to go with it, had the surgery and since have not had to worry about the spasms or the drowsiness of pills.

   As I said before, there are positives of leg spasms. There is the muscle usage, however small it may be. The other being that if you are taking enough medication that you do not usually experience spasms or tightness and you notice they are returning, this could mean that you have some type of irregularity that is irritating your lower half. In my experience this has usually been a urinary tract infection, but there are others. If this happens I recommend checking the skin for cuts or sores, and perhaps seeing a doctor if there are not any problems you can see and the spasms persist.

13) <u>Corner Guards</u>

When rolling around the house daily, it is possible that accidents can occur. One of those accidents is running in to the wall or hitting the corners of walls, whether you are going too fast and cannot stop in time or you turn in an area where there is not enough room. These can cause paint to chip or even pieces of the wall to break off. To prevent this, I have put up plastic corner guards on the corners I go by most often. The guards are clear so they can be seen but do not stand out. I like them because I no longer need to touch up where I have damaged the wall for myself, but also if I ever decide to move and want it to look good to potential buyers. These can be found at any home improvement stores and do not cost very much money.

14) <u>Standing Frame</u>

This is a piece of medical equipment that helps to keep the bones in legs strong by putting weight on them, and helps to hold the leg muscles in a stretch for a long time. It also helps with a condition called lordosis. This is similar to scoliosis in that the spine is curved, except this is a front-to-back curve rather than side-to-side. The frame presses the body from the front and the back, and this helps to straighten the spine. I stand three to four times a week, for about forty-five minutes each time. The length of time and frequency varies between users based on comfort level. Remember that it is important to always do stretches (tip #16) before standing so no muscles are pulled.

  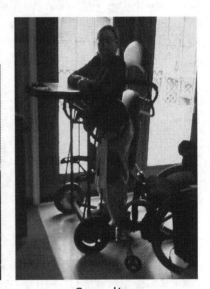

Down   Halfway up   Standing

15) Front-loading Washing Machine

With this doing laundry is much easier because you can reach in the washer to get all the clothing out. This helps back muscles and frustration levels a lot!

16) Stretches & Exercises

It is important to keep the leg, arm and back muscles flexible so they will not be torn.   Even if legs are not being used, stiff muscles can make transferring very difficult. The lower-body muscles need to be limber so no muscles are pulled when doing activities. The stretches one should do regularly are:

a) Calf: Leg bent at knee, foot on opposite thigh, pull foot up towards shin, hold for 10 seconds, let go. Do this three to five times to loosen legs for the day.

b) Hamstring: Leg straight out in front (up on couch or bed), bend upper-half of body forward down towards leg, hold for 15 seconds, rise back up. Again, do this three to five times to fully stretch the bottom thigh muscle.

c) Back/Shoulders: The stretch-band is a high density workout band that can be wrapped around a stable fixture and gives the resistance needed for quality stretches designed by therapists. These are available in different levels of resistance, depending on the strength and needs of the user.

First I wrap the band around a stable fixture like a pole (the bar right under the top of the standing frame is a good choice), then I grab both ends of the band and start the stretches. The stretches of this type one should do regularly are:

Back: Pull straight back, bending at the elbows and hold the stretch for a count of ten, three to five times.

Sides: Pulling straight out to both sides (3 to 5 times for a count of ten).

Another effective method of stretching the back muscles, if you are able, is to bend over at the waist and reach towards the ground. This not only stretches the back muscles, it also helps to lengthen the spine and always makes me feel better.

Exercises–For the first three I use the stretch-band. Repetition of ten.

a) Arms straight out in front of chest: hold fists together and then stretch band out to sides as far as you can.

b) Band around back: stretch out front until arms are straight.

c) Same as exercise b, but up toward the ceiling.

d) Push up into a weight shift. Then let down, then up again for as many times as possible.

e) Push up and swing hips side to side or around in a circular motion. This helps to strengthen the trunk muscles, which are very important for balance. I like to do this when listening to music and dance to the song. I also do push-ups to the beat of the song. This can be a very good workout if the beat is fast. Just be careful not to overdo it. Pulled muscles are no fun!

f) Another exercise to strengthen the trunk muscles is to sit on a bed or couch with arms above head and try to wave them back and forth without falling.

Weights also help to strengthen arms and back muscles. Ask your doctor what they would recommend for your individual needs, or ask for a referral to a physical therapist. They will be able to tell you the specific weights and exercises they believe will help you best.

a) Bicep curls

b) Tricep lifts

c) Arm straight out to side, lift up

d) Down on opposite side, lift up to same side

17) Pillows

I use five or six pillows at night. I have my head pillows of course (one regular and one softer on top of that), but with paralysis there is a need for others. The three or four additional pillows that I use at night include one regular-sized and two or three small pillows:

The regular-sized pillow I put in front of me to lie against. I position the pillow so that the top is against my chest and the bottom is against my abdomen. This helps to prevent the top half of my body rolling over onto my chest while my legs are still turned sideways. That would twist the spine and bend my shoulder forward, causing pain in both areas.

One of the small pillows I put between my knees. This is important so the top bone is not pressing against the bottom bone. It improves circulation, preventing pressure sores, and relieves discomfort and stiffness in the lower back. Luckily, the feeling in my legs helps me know when my leg has fallen asleep. As I said, my legs tingle all the time because blood is flowing normally. I know when an area has no feeling I need to get blood back to it. To do this for the lower half of my bottom leg, I lift it and put my knee on top of the pillow in front of me. Then, after a little while the tingling will start again.

The other one or two small pillows I put under the side of me that is against the bed. My stomach muscles are paralyzed, and because of this I cannot hold myself straight in that area and my side tends to sink down in to the bed. Lying without the pillow under my side will make my hips and ribs touch on the opposite (top) side of the body.

Apart from not being correct for the spine, it is uncomfortable and even painful at times. When I put the pillow(s) under my side it not only takes the weight off that side, but also allows me to stretch the top side. This makes it feel much better. I have found the pillow that works best for me under my side is a neck pillow, like the one pictured on the next page. It is a roll, but also U-shaped. This ensures that it not only fits under my side, but also wraps around my waist for extra support. Over time it begins to break down and does not hold me up as well, but instead of buying a new one that often I put another little pillow under it. I only buy a new pillow when even using both of those will not hold me straight. Then I let my cat have the old ones for her bed and I know she loves it.

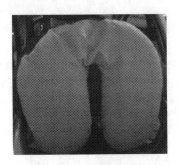

It is also important to make sure that the lower half of the top leg (shin and foot) is not pressed against the same area of the bottom leg. To make sure this doesn't happen to me I have developed a mnemonic method I mentioned earlier. I use the abbreviations TB and BF. To many people these could mean "tuberculosis" and "best friend," but to me they mean "top-back" and "bottom-front." I always make sure the shin/calf/foot on top is behind the one on the bottom, as shown above.

Along with the extra pillows, there is a cushion called an "egg-crate mattress pad" that is helpful in bed. This is a soft foam pad that lays on top of the mattress but under the sheet and has bumps and dips that look like a large egg carton. It helps to reduce pressure and improve the blood flow to prevent sores in people who stay in bed most of the time or cannot move to shift weight on their own at night.

Another pad that is helpful for the mattress is one designed for wetness protection. With paralysis there is a greater risk of the urethra muscle spasming or losing control, so there is a greater chance of an accident. Along with that, urinary tract infections can cause spasms or control loss to become more likely when using catheters. If either one of these causes an accident in bed and there is no protection on the mattress, it can be very unfortunate. I keep one on my bed all the time, on top of the egg-crate mattress under the sheet, just in case. They are available both in plastic and quilted fabric.

18) Air Compressor

Many wheelchair tires have tubes which are filled with air. Like any other air-filled tire, they must always be properly inflated to work well. When they are fully inflated the user does not need to exert as much energy to push themselves. Inflation is also important because the brakes lock against the tires, so tires must always be fully inflated to ensure they work properly. I also have an extra pair of wheels I keep in my trunk of my car in case something ever goes wrong with one or both of mine, whether I am at home or out.

19) Gloves/Socks for Night

After using hands to push around all day they can become hard and leathery, and that makes the skin more likely to crack open. To help this, I used cotton gloves and healing soothing repair cream at night while I was sleeping. Now I still use the cream, but I have found that using socks works even better than the gloves. The fingers of gloves often times wipe the lotion from fingers when sliding them on. Using socks prevents this from happening. I use the small ankle-less socks so I don't need to worry about any extra material.

Sometimes skin becomes so dry that it starts to crack open. It is very hard to heal this because we use our hands so much. If this happens, a remedy is to wear a plastic glove on the hand during the day. This keeps moisture in, and stops any healing cream from being wiped off. You can also use these at night in place of cloth gloves or socks.

20) Sleep

With all the extra effort it takes to do normal activities it often feels like I have been working out all day. Between this and all the medicine I take, I can very tired. Getting up and turning over in the night also makes me lose a little sleep. I don't like napping in the middle of the day, so to prevent this I try to get more sleep at night. It is almost like having some in reserve for when I need it. Every night I plan to get about nine hours in bed, so then I will hopefully get at least eight hours of sleep, i.e. If I know I have to get up at seven the following morning, I try my best to go to bed by ten. I have noticed that getting any extra sleep definitely helps my energy level the next day.

21) Walkie Talkies/Intercoms

As I have said, being in a wheelchair or having another form of a disability that affects the legs makes regular activities more difficult and takes more energy and time. A walkie-talkie or plug-in intercom can help in these instances. If you live with someone and can communicate with them through this instead of getting in your chair and wheeling to them, it is lovely! I speak from personal experience. When I was back in my room but needed something from the front of the house, I loved just being able to push the button and ask my mom if she would bring it to me. You can also call or text the person on your cell phone if you are able, but that takes more time and can cost money on your phone bill.

22) Leggings/T.E.D. Hose

With paralysis, it is difficult to regulate body temperature. Legs more easily become cold because of this, and then may take longer to warm back up. The leggings help to maintain the body heat of the lower limbs. I wear a pair under my pants whenever I think my legs may get cold (in the winter, but also in air-conditioning I cannot control).

Beyond basic leggings, there are medical ones called "T.E.D." hose. This stands for Thrombo-Embolic Deterrent. These are tight, thick, elastic stockings that are used as a preventive measure to reduce the occurrence of emboli or blood clots in the legs. These occur more frequently in those who are not very active, so people with paralysis are especially at risk. When legs do not move blood tends to pool, and this is an environment in which clots can easily form. The hose compress those areas and decrease the chances of those by promoting circulation, and because of this legs stay very warm when using them.

If I put the hose on when my leg(s) are cold, they will warm up in minutes. This helps reinforce how good they are for my circulation and remind me to wear them often. My only warning is to make sure they are on smooth and there are no folds or creases in the material. This causes red dents in the skin that may take some time to go away.

23) Wheels (for undressing)

Getting clothing on and off the lower half can be a difficult task, depending on the level of paralysis. This is my method: I grab the top of my pants (or belt loops, if the pants I am wearing has them) with my thumbs, push up like I am doing a weight shift to get the pants off of my waist and halfway off my bottom, then push forward to get them the rest of the way off my bottom and down my thighs to my knees as the chair rolls forward. It is then much easier to pull the pants the rest of the way off. If you are not able to use the above method, the toilet and the bed are good places both for dressing and undressing the lower half.

24) Leg Movement

There are electronic stimulation devices that help to prevent atrophy in the muscles. The bike is expensive, but works very well. I learned about it when I went to Washington University's rehabilitation program in St. Louis.

There are electrodes that attach to the upper leg (top and bottom) and gluteus muscles, and then stimulate them to help pedal the bike. I am not able to do the whole process on my own, so for help I call the university near my house and speak to the physical therapy department. There are always students there who are happy to come help me, often without charge, for the experience. After they help me they are able to include that on their résumé, and I am happy to provide a reference for them.

Steps:

1) Warm-up stretches (helpers #16).

2) Transfer on to the bike.

3) Strap feet in to the cushioned pedal boots and wrap the thigh holding fixtures around the thighs and then velcro in place.

4) Adhere the electrodes to quadriceps, hamstrings, and gluteal muscles.

5) Helper cycles the bike manually using the handle on the side of the boot for one minute.

6) The stimulation starts and powers the leg muscles to cycle the bike on their own. Until legs are strong enough to pedal the bike alone for an extended time, the helper needs to help the legs cycle.

7) When the legs are unable to cycle on their own, the bike stops the stimulation. Then cycle the bike manually for two minutes for cool down.

8) Take off thigh holders and electrodes, unstrap feet, and go relax!

25) Other People

As I have learned over the years, it is not possible to do everything myself. At first I was self-conscious about accepting help because I did not want anyone to think that I could not do whatever I was trying on my own. I have now gotten past that and realized there are things I need to do that I can't do myself or are just much easier with someone else's help.

Beyond helping with tasks and chores, other people are good for sharing thoughts with and getting all of my feelings out. This includes not just the bad, but also the good. Many hospitals and rehabilitation facilities have group therapy sessions every week where people can go and get their feelings out and share stories. People can also share tips they have learned and their methods of doing activities, just as I am doing through this book.

26) Forearms

These can be efficient brakes if I'm going too fast or if I'm not able to put on the chair brakes. Just know that stopping too fast could make you fall out of the chair. When stopping be sure to use both arms. If you are going too fast and only use one arm, you may only spin in a circle and fall!

27) Wheelchair (and Pharmacy) Technician

It is beneficial to become friends with the people at the local wheelchair store and repair shop. I always have their number available in case something goes wrong with my chair and I need their help. When I call my local repair shop and say that it's Jessie calling, they know it's me without me having to say my last name! This is not because my chairs are low-quality, but because I am hard on them. This is also true of my pharmacy because I am on so many medications!

28) Pocket Doors

Traditional swinging doors can be difficult to open and close when in a wheelchair. A solution to this is a 'pocket door.' These doors open by sliding back into an opening in the wall. With these there is never a struggle with opening the door and backing up little by little, and never one with reaching behind or rolling backwards to shut the door little by little. When I go through regular doors, I reach my fingers back through the hinge slot and push it enough that I can close it using the knob. Sometimes it shuts too fast and can hurt, but it works most of the time.

29) Weight Shifts

Weight shifts are when one pushes up or rolls to one side to get more blood to a part of the body that they have been putting weight on for a long time. I do these in my chair by locking my brakes and pushing up so that my arms are straight and my bottom is not on the seat anymore. My physical therapists at the hospital told me to try to do one of these every hour for at least one minute. With time I have found I do not need to every hour, but I still do them often. I have also found that staying "up" for a longer time is better. This also feels good because it helps to stretch the spine.

It is important to do the weight shifts because they help to prevent pressure sores, which can occur when too much weight is put on a specific area of the body for too long and blood cannot circulate freely to reach that area. These sores are dangerous because they require much maintenance and could even require a hospital visit or stay, depending on the severity. I have had one instance of this, on my left hip, but I simply stopped putting weight on that side for about one month and it went away. It was unpleasant for me because I like to fall asleep on my left side. However, it did teach me a lesson and now I am very careful because I do not want to have that experience again!

To help combat any issues at night, as I said, I try to put equal weight on both sides. I start the night sleeping on my left side, and then when I wake up in the middle of the night I turn and sleep on my right side. I'm pretty sure that sleeping on one side all night would not cause any problems, but I believe it is better to be safe than sorry.

30) <u>Vocational Rehabilitation Services</u>

The goal of V.R. (what I have abbreviated the name to over the years, as well as voc. rehab.) is to help a disabled person find a career that they would enjoy doing, help them achieve the skills needed for that and then help them find a job in that field. If education is needed to achieve that job, they can also help pay school expenses.

Another positive aspect of the vocational rehabilitation services is that the client is able to work one-on-one with a counselor. This helps to ensure that anything to do with my case or anything I tell them is strictly between them. My counselor was very helpful to me through my whole education. If I should ever need to look for a job, I know that my counselor will be ready and very helpful in my career achievement.

31) <u>Animal Aides</u>

There are disabled people who do not need help and others that need full-time assistance, but there are also many cases between those. One option for these cases is an animal helper. Animals such as capuchin monkeys, dogs, miniature horses and parrots can help people with many different disabilities. You may wonder why someone would want to use a miniature horse in place of a seeing-eye dog. Allergies is one reason, but some people say that they are more mild-mannered, trainable and less threatening than large dogs. Horses are also used in programs that help people regain self-esteem and confidence.

Beyond helping the blind, dogs are good aides for retrieving things around the house. They can even learn sign language commands. This also goes for monkeys, plus they are smaller and more agile than dogs. Parrots can be used in therapy for the mentally disabled. More information on any of these can be found on the internet, or at a local rehabilitation or therapy center.

32) Notes at Night

When I am going to sleep at night, or in the middle of the night after I have been sleeping, I often think of things I need to do the next day. For this, I did keep a notebook next to my bed. When I would think of these things I would turn on my bedroom light, write down the note and then turn off the light. I have since discovered that I can instead write a text message, and then not send it. When I do this, the phone automatically saves the message in my drafts. Then, the following morning I am able to look at those messages. I can also send the message to my email to see the next day when I open it.

This is good for multiple reasons. I do not have to turn on the light so I will not wake anyone if they are sleeping in the same room, and I know I will not lose the message like I could have when I was writing on a piece of paper. I can write lists of things that need to be remembered in an email and then save it in my drafts, or just write it in a document and save.

33) Oops! (Methods of reseating)*

There have been times when I could not make a transfer, or something else has caused me to fall out of my chair, and then I was on the floor. Luckily, none of these was a violent fall. They were more like "slumps."

I think in my head:
- Here I go. I'm going to do a transfer.
- Move each leg out a little and position feet.
- Push up.
- Push over.
- Okay, almost there.
- Uh-oh, starting to slip.
- No, no, no. I can still do it.
- Okay, no I can't.
- Okay, now I am on the floor.
- Then I at least smile, if not laugh.

If I do happen to fall and no one is there to help me back into my chair, I try to find a flat surface (like a low table, chair or couch without the cushion) onto which I am able to transfer. From there, it is much easier to transfer back into my chair. If there is no low flat surface that I am able to use, this is the method that I have learned (and used) that I hope other people will be able to use as well:

1) Take the cushion off of the chair.

2) Slide the cushion under the footplate of the chair.

3) Turn so your back is facing the chair.

4) Pull up so that your bottom is on cushion, then on the footplate (if it is wide enough).

5) Reach up behind and fix your hands onto the chair frame where it bends to go down to the footplate.

6) Pull your body up onto the chair seat.

7) Transfer out of the chair and put the cushion back on.

* Please practice with supervision before attempting alone. Rehab therapists can help in the achievement of this or a different method of getting back in the chair.

34) Hobbies and Interests

It is easy to feel very limited or discouraged by paralysis, but there are many activities that don't involve the use of legs. It is important to find fun activities and pursue those, and then to share them with others.

One of the hobbies that I enjoy is making picture collages on my computer. I have included some at the end of the book. To do this I use my cell phone, but it could also be done with a digital camera that is able to be connected to a computer or pictures found on the internet and saved to the computer. My method of creating these collages is only four steps:

1) I take the picture with my phone.

2) I send the picture as a text message to my email address.

3) When I get the text message email, I open it and then save the picture(s) to my computer.

4) Finally, I open my Iworks word processor program (or Microsoft Word, if that is your program) and insert the pictures in the size and pattern I think works the best.

I do this on my computer because it is much easier than cutting actual pictures and gluing them on paper, but also because I can add colors or fancy writing if I want and email them to whomever I want.

I also watch sports. My two favorites are football and NASCAR. I had always paid attention to football and racing, but when I was home after my accident I started watching them more. It was (and is) nice to look forward to the games/races every weekend, and exciting to watch them.

I live in Indianapolis so of course I like the Colts, but as you know my favorite team in the NFL is the Green Bay Packers. Of course I like Brett Favre because he was such a great quarterback, but my favorite player was the running back Ahman Green. I love the team now as well. They are amazing players and I can't wait to see how each game will go!

My favorite Pack players now are Aaron Rodgers and Clay Matthews. I wear my green Rodgers jersey when they play at home, and my white Matthews jersey when they are away. I have a whole wall of my house devoted to them. I am a true Packers fan, and I am proud to show it to anyone and everyone I can!

Of course I love the Packers for their playing and skill of the game, but as I said at the beginning of the book I love the outlook and quotes of Vince Lombardi. The way he looked at the game is I'm sure also the way he looked at life: be positive and to believe in yourself. If you do not have confidence in yourself, look deep and you will find that you can do it. Once you find that confidence, do not let it go. Know that you have it in you to do what you want and need to do.

I would love to meet the team now and tell them how great they are and how happy they have made me many game days in the past, and I can't wait for all the game days yet to come. I might also ask them to thank me for some of their wins. When I am watching the games, I often yell to the players through my television telling them what to do. When they do what I have said, they most always pick up yards, score and win the game. I know it is silly, but I bet it made a couple of my readers smile and that is my mission.

As I said, I also watch NASCAR. My favorite driver in that sport is Dale Earnhardt, Jr. I like how he races his car. I think he learned a lot from his father, but then branched out and made his style his own. I think this is how we should all live: look to people for guidance and examples, but then simply use those to find our own style. Of course I would also love to meet him, tell him this and thank him for all the great races I've seen!

Bathroom Activities
Using the facilities & Cleaning up

These are some of the tips I have learned over the years about "going to the bathroom" that have helped me, and I hope can help others. It is important to talk to your doctor or therapist about all of my activities and suggestions to make sure they agree what is safe and most effective for every individual.

Toilet Tools

Stationary grab bar I use at my mom's house

As I said, the easiest way to transfer on and off of the toilet is to use a 'grab bar.' This is a bar that is attached to the wall on one side of the toilet and helps provide stability. To transfer, I roll in front of the toilet and lock my brakes so that I am sideways/diagonal in front/side of the toilet facing the grab bar. Then I reach across, "grab" the bar and pull myself over. Then when I am done I can push against it to get back in to my chair. There are also bars that are hinged and able to be folded up against the wall when you do not need them.

I also have a portable handle with strong suction cups that can be used as a grab bar when there are none in the bathroom you wish to use. These can be found at many medical supplies stores or online.

The location chosen for the bar depends on the stability of (or stud location in) the walls, the layout of the bathroom and preference. I am now able to use grab bars (or anything else that is stationary and strong enough to put weight on) on both sides of the toilet, but this is only after much practice.

It is important to always have someone with you when you try new activities like this. Make sure that you are able to do the transfer, or any other potentially dangerous activity, many times before attempting alone.

If more support and stability than just the grab bar on the single side of the toilet is needed, there are support rails with grips on both sides. They are available for permanent placement, but there are also lightweight and easy–fold options just like the bars. These can be found in medical care catalogs or stores. No matter what your needs may be, you will be able to find the perfect one through those.

I have found the bar also helps when dressing my lower half. I pull the pants over my lower legs and past my knees and then as I pull myself to the right it takes the weight off the left side and makes it much easier to pull the pants up there, just as in bed. When the pants are up farther on that side, it is then easier to pull them up on the other side. I alternate sides until I have pulled the pants up all the way.

After I have transferred over to the toilet, I do not move my chair. I leave it in front/next to the toilet. This saves time and helps in the process. Trying to insert the catheter with both legs down and pushed together on the toilet seat can be very difficult. I know that it is much easier for me if I leave my foot up on the chair cushion so that I have more space.

To insert the catheter, I must lean back. On certain toilet lids this can be very uncomfortable and even painful. One trick that I thought of was to put padding on the bottom of the toilet seat lid. It is very easy to find soft foam padding at any fabric or hobby store. My mom cut the foam into a square. The best cover for the foam is a pillowcase. I tuck the end of the pillowcase inside itself so it is only half the length it was before and then slide it over the foamed lid. It is a perfect fit on most all lids, and I can wash it whenever I want.

If an adaptation of the toilet seat is needed, or wanted, these can also be found in many medical supply stores or catalogs. There are pads that can be put on the seat to soften it, and others to elevate it. There are even risers that can be adhered to the bottom of the seat, if the user would like to still use the original one.

I have learned that it is better to have a snap-on toilet seat/lid than one that is fixed. When transferring and getting pants off and on, there is much side-to-side movement that affects the seat of the toilet. With this movement on a fixed seat, one could completely snap the seat and lid off, and then they would need to buy a new one to replace it. With the snap-on there is less worry of that. These are sold wherever other toilet seats are.

For "cathing" (my slang for using the catheter), I need a flat surface near the toilet to keep my accessories on. When I am staying with my mom I use one of her chairs with a towel laid over it. With the catheters, gloves and lubrication gel I also keep a bag of wet wipes and extra underwear just in case I ever need it.

The flat surface only needs to be large enough to hold these items. As my bathroom had to be rebuilt after a fire, I was able to make it more "user-friendly." The shelves I had before were high and not very deep. It was hard to fit everything that I needed, and to see and reach what was on the top shelf. The new positioning is lower and deeper. This ensures I am able to fit all of my supplies on the shelves and have easy access to all of them.

New shelves in remodeled bathroom
(The opening on the floor is where my new toilet will be)

* Side note*: I have found that I usually do not need the whole large wet wipe, so when I buy the large bag of wet wipes at the store I take out a small stack at a time and cut those in half so they are squares instead of rectangles. By doing this the bag lasts twice as long. I always wash my hands before I do this, and the scissors I use are strictly for the bathroom. I then store the wipes in a gallon-sized freezer or storage plastic bag. I only take out a small stack at a time and store those in a sandwich or quart-sized plastic bag.

<u>#1</u> :)

Most all paraplegics use catheters to urinate. The therapists and nurses at the hospital taught me how to do this. They instructed me to first put on the powder-free vinyl gloves, put a little lubricating jelly on to a piece of toilet paper, clean the area around my urethra with an antibacterial wipe, dab the catheter into the jelly, and then insert the catheter into my urethra to let the urine come out. I have found that as long as I am sure to wash my hands well with soap, I do not need to wear the gloves. I now only use them for the other "toilet activity" (#2, ha-ha).

I then clean the area with the wet wipe. Over the years I have discovered that I do not need to put the lubrication jelly onto the toilet paper separately. The opening of the lubricant tube is often a small round hole just big enough to insert the end of the catheter, so I am able to cover it by doing that. In some cases, there is enough natural lubrication in the area one does not even need to use extra.

After I have done this, I insert the catheter and wait for my bladder to empty. When it seems that I have stopped, I pull the catheter out a little. I have also found over the years that if I push the catheter back to where it was before, any urine that was not released the first time will then be.

Catheters

I order my catheters through a mail-order company. The ones that I use are 14 french (this is the diameter measurement of the catheters), six inches long and are clear plastic. They are individually wrapped and are stored together in a cardboard box.

When I first get the catheters, I unwrap them individually. I then cut the funnel off of the end using my bathroom scissors. After I have done that, I put them all into a fresh sandwich or quart freezer bag. This makes accessing and storing them easier because you do not need to unwrap a catheter every time you use one, and because they take up much less room without the funnels.

The catheter maker recommends throwing them away after only a single use, but I have found that if I wash them with antibacterial dish soap I am able to use them more than once. I now get one box of thirty catheters a month. After using the catheters, I store them in a container until I am ready to wash them.

The steps of my cleaning method:

1) I clean the sink and soak catheters in warm soapy water for about forty-five minutes.

2) With clean hands, I move (swirl) the caths around through the water (a couple at a time) until I am sure they have all had a thorough cleaning, putting the clean ones on the towel as I go.

3) After they have all been cleaned, I turn on the hot water and rinse three or four at a time very well until sure all the soap is out.

4) When they have all been rinsed I shake most all the water out, three or four at a time, over the bathtub or shower floor.

5) I lay them out on one half of the towel (regular-size, folded in half long-way) individually so they are not touching each other. Again, they take up much less space without the funnel on the end.

6) I cover them with the other half of the towel, wash the holder and lid, lay those on the towel and allow all to dry.

7) After they have all dried, I am able to put them back into the bag and use them all one or two more times (after that, the material starts to break down and using them is too difficult).

#2 (aka: "Bowel Program")

The supplies I use for this are powder-free vinyl gloves and lubricating gel. When I was in the hospital, the therapists taught me what they called a bowel program. This was a schedule of when I should "go number 2" and the supplies I should use when I do. They told me that because I was now paralyzed I would not always know when I needed to go like other people do. Many people do not need to go every day, depending on how their digestion works. To learn your schedule start with every day, then every other day, and so on until you are familiar with your body and its digestive system.

Hint: When you pass gas, often times it means that you need to go to the bathroom (Like your body is trying to get your attention-"psst." Ha-ha). Another hint your body can give you is spasms. When I have jump spasms in just one of my legs, it is sometimes because I need to go (pressing against the colon causes irritation and makes the leg spasm).

Showering

Chair or bench

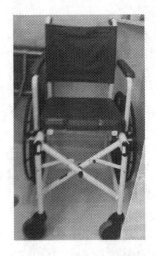 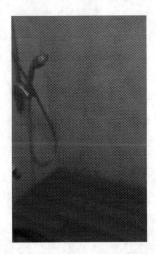

One of these two is necessary for showering. I personally prefer the shower chair because I feel that it holds me in better and gives me extra security. We had already installed the bench at my parents' house before I decided that, so I used the one above for a time. Depending on your level of paralysis, you can either get a standard model shower chair or one customized for your needs. Also, the middle of the seat can be removed if preferred.

Hand-held shower sprayer and Threshold

Doing tasks without help is important to me, and because of this I learned how to work with adaptive showering devices. One of these is the hand-held sprayer. Since I could no longer stand and turn in the shower, I could not properly rinse all areas of my body. I found this provides the control that the regular shower head does not. I am able to spray the water where I want when I want, and turn the sprayer away when I do not want the water on me.

There are also long-handle brushes and sponges for use when washing the back and any other hard-to-reach areas. With these you can cleanse and exfoliate, while at the same time gently massaging the area. There are also lotion applicators with long handles which can be found in the same catalogs or stores as those.

A very helpful tool for the shower is a 'threshold.' This is a flexible strip of rubber or plastic that runs along floor of the entrance to a roll-in shower and prevents water from streaming out onto the bathroom floor. It is a must!

My Chair
Parts that help me, and may help others

I have had three chairs over the years of my paralysis. I got my first chair when I was still in the hospital. I eventually grew out of it, mainly because the back was higher than I needed. My second chair had a lower back and wider footplate (in case I had an "oops"). I had this chair for a long time too, but I was having so much pain that I had a wheelchair evaluation done to figure out which features I did and did not need. At the evaluation they determined that my rib and abdominal muscles could not hold me up straight, and because of this I was experiencing muscle strain and curvature. They told me I needed a chair with high side guards that would hold me up and lessen my pain.

Below are some pictures of my new chair, along with explanations of its features:

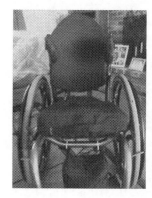  

The first picture is my chair from the front. It shows how narrow the chair back must be compared to the chair's lower half in order for the side guards to properly hold me up under my arms and not allow too much "give" from side to side. This picture also shows the bar in front that holds one of my bags. This bag is where I keep valuable things, such as my wallet and car keys, because it cannot be easily accessed by other people.

My high side guards hold me up straight but can be folded out when I need, as you can see in the middle picture. There is a slope of my seat from front to back, called "dump," which helps me to feel secure in the chair. If the seat was level from front to back, there would be a much greater chance of falling and I would be afraid to do all the things I do now. The incline of my chair is not very great. It varies from person to person due to their comfort level. The wheelchair retailers can adjust this on "test" chairs until they find the correct level for the user.

The third picture is the rear of the chair. I chose a solid Jay back for this chair because my previous chair did not have a solid back, and this was another reason for my pain. This hard back allows no give from front to back, which is the support I need. In this picture you can also see the bar on the back of my chair. This is what anyone else uses to pick up the chair, and where I hang my other bag. This bag is for things I use often, such as my hand lotion and cell phone, because it is easier for me to reach behind to get things than to bend down forward to get them.

On my chair I use a Jay J2 cushion. It has a regular thick pad cushion (dark gray), but also a layer on top (light gray) which contains a thin pad in the front half and gel in the back half. The gel is good because it takes the shape of what is on it, which in this case are my gluteal muscles. :) It helps by relieving pressure and allowing blood to flow better. It is also more comfortable than the solid cushions I had in the past.

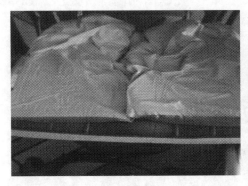 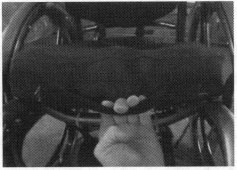

My cushion cover has a strap on the front of the cover. This allows the cushion to be easily taken off and fixed back into place on the seat of the chair. The other key reason for the cover is that it and the seat of the chair both have Velcro on them. The soft Velcro is on the bottom edge of the cushion cover, and the hook Velcro is sewn on to the seat. This way I know that the cushion will always be in its correct place on the chair.

More features:

In the first picture you can see the brakes of my chair. These are very easy to push down and pull up in that location, and they hold very well as long as my tires are fully aired up.

You can also see my foot-strap in this picture. It helps to keep my feet on the foot-plate, but is fabric and adjustable so I am able to change the length if I want or need.

The other picture shows my footplate and the textured pad that I put on it after I got the chair. Before, the plate was smooth metal and my feet easily slid off of it. Since we put this textured no-slip pad on, my feet do not slip. The pads can be found with outdoor supplies. They are meant to be adhered to the bottom of heavy objects so that they will not slip, but we improvised this new use for them and it works very well!

I also use anti-tip bars. They are accessories on the back of the wheelchair to keep it from falling over backward. Part of the goal of physical therapy involves balancing and is directed at making the patient strong and comfortable enough to remove these, depending on injury level. I have heard them jokingly called "sissy bars" by people who do not need them on their chair anymore, because the bars are much like training wheels on a bicycle. I am almost sure that I would be okay without them, but I like the extra safety. Over the years I have also found that leaning the chair back on the bars helps to take the weight off my spine, so because of this I now call them my "recliner bars." Just be sure to not lean back too far or the chair may fall over backward!

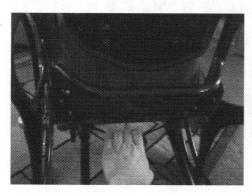

In these pictures you can see how I am able to break down my chair. The first step is removing the cushion. After that I use the drawstring shown in the first picture to fold the back down flat, as shown in the second picture. As you can see, my side guards are affixed just high enough that they do not interfere with the back laying flat again the seat. If the chair needs to be broken down more than this to fit into a car or small area, the wheels are easily removed and the anti-tip bars can be flipped up or removed.

Since I took the first pictures of my chair, I have decorated the back. I did not have any stickers for a long time, then I decided to make it my own. I really like it, and I get many compliments and laughs from people who also like it!

Top sticker: FOXY RIDER

Others: CATCH ME IF YOU CAN,

3 Green Bay stickers,

Harley Davidson logo and joker girl,

both on glitter paper.

Out & About
Leaving, driving, and returning

Inside-Out Socks

The toe area of shoes can sometimes be cramped and most all socks have a seam running over the toes which can dig in if this occurs, especially for long periods of time. I noticed this happening to me. I am not sure if this was hurting me but I do not like to take chances with my lower half, so now I always wear my socks inside-out.

Gloves for Day

"Wheelchair hands" get a big workout every day, so wearing good gloves is important. They work to not dirty hands or cause calluses when wheeling around during day. I have found that bicycle gloves work very well for this. There are fingerless gloves, as well as regular.

Hand-driving Supplies

Many people believe that if someone's legs don't work they either cannot drive, or have to buy a special car. Neither of these is true. There are accessories that can be added to a regular car to make it "hand-drivable." These tools are not only used by paralyzed people, but also by amputees and other people who for any reason cannot use their legs to drive.

The main accessory for hand-driving is the hand control for the accelerator and brake pedals. The control is a rod with one end affixed to the steering wheel and the other above the pedals. The rod is attached so that when the driver pulls the handle down toward themselves the gas pedal is pushed, and when they push forward the brake pedal is pushed. It does take time and practice, but over time becomes easier to control just like driving with feet.

The second of the accessories is a 'pedal lock,' also known as a 'pedal guard.' This is a stable fixture drilled in to the floor of the car that covers the gas pedal and prevents any accidental pedal pushing. There is usually not a worry for this when transferring in and out of the car because it is off or in park, but there is a chance when moving around in the car once it is running or a leg spasm occurring that causes the foot to push the pedal down.

The final accessory for driving with hands is a 'spinner knob.' These are needed for steering a car when the driver cannot use both hands. The knob itself spins, and this makes turning with only one hand much easier for the driver. They are available in different shapes and colors depending on the user's needs and preferences.

Baskets for out

Baskets and carts are great when getting things at stores, but my problem was what to do when I got everything I had bought home. Taking bags of groceries in one at a time is very monotonous and tiring, and my house basket is not very big. One day I asked the manager at my local store if he would allow me to take one of their baskets home with me and explained why. He said that would be fine, so now I have my own. It is so great being able to bring everything I have bought in to my house in just one or two trips.

The other problem with using random baskets at stores is that they are often dirty. People set the basket down in the parking lot when they were done, and then I would need to carry that basket on my lap. Yuck. I cleaned the bottom of my basket the first time I brought it home. Now I keep it in the trunk of my car and use it at all stores. Though I do get strange looks when I am at a different store than the name on my basket. Ha-ha!

Cloths and Soap

Wheels can become very dirty after being out, so I wash my tires to help prevent the floors of my house from becoming dirty. Luckily I have a bathroom right off my garage, so this is easy. To do this, I get one corner of the cloth wet and soapy. I use that to scrub the dirt off of the tire. Another corner I just get wet and wipe off the soap (dry tires collect dirt and pet hair if there is any soap residue left on them). I then dry the tires with the other end of the cloth. If you prefer, you can use two cloths for this: one for washing and wiping, and the other for drying. If you do this, you can then use the drying cloth for the washing and wiping the next time.

I also keep a towel in my car for wiping my wheels before putting them in the car. I wipe the wheels with the underside of the towel to do this because I have found that the underside threading collects dirt and anything else that is on the wheel better than the "smooth" side. I then lay the towel across my lap, smooth (clean) side down, so I don't get my pants dirty as I pull the chair over me. I also lay the towel over my lap before getting the chair back out if I think the wheels may be still be dirty.

Para-Perks
The bright side

This is my mom with Grace & me with Nadyne

I believe that everyone should try to find the good in any situation. These are the positive points that I have discovered throughout the years of my paralysis:

1) Closer to animals!

2) Always have somewhere to sit!

3) Get to park up front, and sit up front at many places!

4) People enjoy helping, so allowing them to help makes them feel good about themselves. Getting the help is just a little bonus (Ha-ha). I am also always sure to ask people if there is anything I can do to help them.

5) In some cases the government will pay supplemental security income to people with disabilities. This helps during rehabilitation when not able to work, and if an injury is so serious that someone is not able to work even after rehabilitation.

6) As I said, vocational rehabilitation services are very helpful in finding a job and in achieving the skills for that job.

7) Learning from experiences. Though the manner is unfortunate, many people who go through hard times often learn what they believe is "truly important" in life. Through this book I am conveying what I have learned, hoping to help others with it.

Best Medicine
Finding the Joy

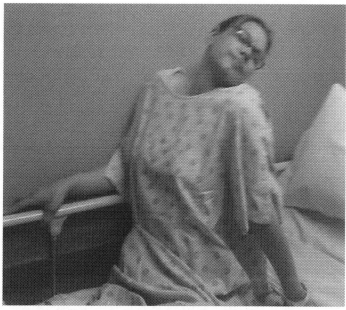

A little hospital gown modeling before surgery

I believe it's important to stay positive, keep a sense of humor and find joy wherever you can. These are some things that have made me laugh over the years, and might make you also:

Personal funnies

• Someone comes home at the end of the day after working hard, sits or lies down and says: "Man, I feel like I got hit by a Mack truck!"

I say: "No, I do! Ha-ha!"

• Now when I am wrong about something and someone tells me, I say: "I sit corrected" (instead of "stand corrected").

• When I go to a restaurant or anywhere that has a chair for a person to sit in, I can move it and say: "Oh thanks, but I brought my own!"

• I tell people my job is 'professional sitter' and then say: "As you can see, I am very committed."

Television

• I like parodies of people with disabilities on television. Something can only offend us if we allow it. I cannot speak for anyone but myself, but the way actors exaggerate and add their own comedy to the disabled characters they play often brings a smile to my face. My favorite is "The Adventures of Handi Man from "In Living Color." He played a superhero that solved problems and helped people in his own special way. At the end of every skit after he had helped the person he would say: "Never underestimate the powers of the handicapped."(8)

Commercials

• For lawyers:

1) They ask: "Were you injured in a car accident?"

I get to answer: "Yes."

2) An actor says: "I was injured in a serious car accident."

I say: "Me too!"

They say: "Now I use a wheelchair."

I say: "Me too!"

• For back pain remedies:

"The average person sits for eight hours a day."

I say: "Well I am above average!"

• For shoe inserts:

"Do you have back pain?"

I say: "Yes."

"Does it control your life?"

I say: "Yes."

"Try these inserts in your shoes. They make walking easier and more comfortable."

I say: "Well, what if you can't walk?"

They don't answer me. Ha–ha!

Songs

• The ZZ top song "Legs" (9), the line "She's got legs, she knows how to use them"

> I sing: "I've got legs, you know I can't move them"

• The Genesis song "That's All" (10), line "I can't feel a thing from my head down to my toes"

> I sing: "I can't move a thing from my waist down to my toes"

Wordplay–These have made me giggle over the years:

• When I do something that was difficult, I say: "See, I'm not handicapped. I'm handi-capable!"

• Sit

> After I have been up in my chair for a while my back will start hurting and I know I need to get out of my wheelchair and in my recliner, I will say: "Man, I really need to go sit down!"

> When I realize what I have just said I laugh!

• Walk

> 1) A friend will ask me if I want to walk down to the store real quick.
> I say: "No."
> They ask why not.
> I pretend to be a little sad, and say: "Because I can't walk!"

> 2) I was wearing a sweatshirt and was getting hot.
> My friend said: "You better take that off. You don't want to walk around with a red face all day."
> I said: "That won't be a problem!"

3) Joke to tell a friend:

"I went to jail!"

They ask why.

"I was pulled over, and the officer thought I was drunk."

"Why did they think that?"

"Because I couldn't walk a straight line!"

- Run

    "Did you run into him (asking if I saw him)?"

    "No!"

- Kick

    1) Deciding on something:

    "Are you kicking the idea around?"

    "No!"

    2) Death:

    "Ha-ha! I am never going to die!"

    "Why not?"

    "I can't kick, so I will never kick the bucket!"

    I know the wordplays are a little cheesy, but that is the point! It is important to have fun and enjoy your life!

<u>-Ations</u>
Getting the most out of life

I remember thinking that my life was over because I was paralyzed. I thought that because I was in the chair I would not be able to go anywhere or do anything without it being a huge chore, let alone have a successful and happy life. I have since learned that things are a bit more difficult due to the paralysis, but it is by no means a life-ender!

Honestly, if I could go back and change anything that happened in my past I would not. While I don't like all the stress and heartache my family and I had to go through, if I had not gone through all that I have I would not be who I am today. I have grown very much as a person through all of my experiences. Most of all, as I said before, I feel that I have learned what is truly important in life and how to best enjoy it. Moreover, I would not have been able to write this book and hopefully help many people through it.

It is important to not lose dreams, or 'aspirations,' even when the world may seem flipped upside down. They can be put to the side while dealing with issues that are more important, but then they must be revived when those are taken care of and fulfilled.

An example of this is my study of Spanish. I love the language. It is very beautiful and is not a hard language to learn. I also like that it is very similar to Italian, so it is almost like learning two languages at once. I had taken Spanish classes in middle school and high school, but I still wanted to work with it after I graduated.

To do this, I enrolled in Indiana University Purdue University Indianapolis, IUPUI for short. It took six years of daily commuting and hard work, but I did get my degree in Spanish Education. Though I have since decided against that profession, I do not regret the choice of that major at all and am proud of myself for getting the degree. I believe that with my knowledge of Spanish I will be able to reach and hopefully help many more people.

My ultimate dream is to help people to adjust to new circumstances and find the strength that is inside them to move on with their lives and be happy. I have a smaller dream of being a runway model. I think I could roll down the runway, push up to show off what I was wearing, then spin around and roll back up. I would be breaking down barriers for other people and having fun!

Finally, I like home remodel shows and I was thinking that perhaps I could do one or more of my own. I would like to go to the house of a person who for any reason is now in a wheelchair, look around their house and help them decide what would work best for them. I would then have workers remodel a room or two in their house. While I am at their house I could also offer any other tips I have and of course give them a copy of my book. The other benefit of the show would be people watching it would be able to get ideas for their own homes.

I just need help getting the idea off the ground. I know that Oprah Winfrey and Ellen Degeneres love to help people, so perhaps they could help me with both the modeling and the show. I hope that because I speak Spanish I would also be able to do a remodel in a home in which that is the primary language spoken.

I am not sure if any of these will ever happen, but that is why they are called dreams.

To work toward our dreams we must have 'motivation.' We all need that driving force to help us achieve our goals. What helps us to both become and stay motivated is 'inspiration.' The main sources of influence that inspires us are the dream itself and those around us who show the confidence they have in us. Beside those there are other sources of inspiration, and I believe that music is a main one of those.

Music has helped me to get through the hard times, and to enjoy the good times even more. It has the power to make us feel better when nothing else will, and put our feelings into words when we cannot. The music of the song can perk us up when we are doing things or just sitting around, but there are also songs whose words can lift us up when we are at our lowest. I have included a list of lyric quotes at the end of this section that I believe people who have been through hard times can especially relate to and can inspire us in moving on from those times.

To keep working toward the goal when it is difficult and may seem far away we must have a firmness of purpose, or 'determination.' Remember the goal and how good you will feel once it has been reached, as well as how good you will feel about yourself for reaching it. We must devote ourselves completely and wholeheartedly to the process, and have the 'dedication' that will not let us give up even when it may seem very difficult or even impossible.

When we stay determined and dedicated we can achieve the goal, or have dream 'realization.' With this comes a feeling of happiness, or 'gratification.' There is much of this in the rehabilitation process. There were very many goals to fulfill and skills to achieve just to live a normal life after my accident due to my paralysis. These ranged from simply sitting up on my own and balancing to showering and dressing myself. When I learned these things and achieved these goals I felt very good about myself. This joy and self-confidence made me eager to move to the next and see what else I could accomplish.

Another '-Ation' that comes with accomplishing a goal is 'congratulation.' Whenever I achieved a goal that was set for me, the therapists and those close to me would congratulate me for that. I would thank them, and then I would congratulate myself. There is a big difference between being proud of yourself and being arrogant. When I successfully achieve a goal or do something that is difficult, I often congratulate myself. I will say, in my head or out loud, "I make this look good!"

"So many of our dreams at first seem impossible, then they seem improbable, and then, when we summon the will, they soon become inevitable." (11)

> – Christopher Reeve,
> Actor and quadriplegic

Inspirational & Instructional

- "Already Gone" by the Eagles (12)

    The song is about a man leaving his mate before she breaks up with him, but I like to think of it as leaving the bad feelings behind and achieving my goals.

    "So often times it happens that we live our lives in chains, and we never even know we have the key"

    Do not let yourself become trapped in sorrow. You have the power to turn things around and enjoy your life.

- "Trenchtown Rock" by Bob Marley (13)

    "One good thing about music, when it hits you feel no pain"

    It is nice to get lost in a song. We can forget about the bad things for a little while and just enjoy.

- "If Today Was Your Last Day" by Nickelback (14)

  This is a song about making the most of your time and not being caught up in little things that can make you unhappy. It is important to let bad feelings go and concentrate on what can help you achieve the goals that will make your life what you want it to be.

  "What's worth the prize is always worth the fight"

  Achieving a goal can be very difficult, but it is important to keep working and remember the outcome will be what you want and will be worth it.

- "Dynamite" by Taio Cruz (15)

  "I wanna celebrate and live my life"

  Life is a gift, so we need to celebrate every single day.

  In this song he also sings of letting go. I think he means that we should get rid of bad feelings and be peaceful.

- "We Will Rock You/We Are The Champions" by Queen (16)

  "We Will Rock You" is just an awesome pump-up song. It is about making your mark in the world and is very motivational.

  The second part of the song is a look back. I think he is singing that he feels he was punished for something he never did. This is how I feel about disabilities: whether someone is born with one, has an accident or develops one it is never the fault of the person. Times can be very tough, but we still need to work through it and move on.

  "We'll keep on fighting 'til the end"

  Do not give up. Never let a misfortune take over your life. Everyone deserves to live a happy life!

- "Don't Stop" by Fleetwood Mac (17)

  "It'll be better than before, yesterday's gone"

  As I said, the past cannot be changed. Dwelling on misfortunes will only upset you. Concentrate on the future and making your life better.

- "Superman" by Five For Fighting (18)

  He is singing of the difficulties in his life, but that he is proud of his ability to overcome them. It is not easy to deal with the things we do, so we should feel good for being able to do so.

  "I'm more than a bird...I'm more than a plane"

  This speaks to me about rising above troubles and being strong.

- "I'm In A Hurry (And Don't Know Why)" by Alabama (19)

  "I rush and rush until life's no fun"

  This draws attention to the fact that the majority of people seem to be so busy trying to get ahead that they can't enjoy what they already have. It is important to work toward what you want, but it is more important to not get so lost in that pursuit that you are unhappy.

- "Peace Of Mind" by Boston (20)

  "I don't care if I get left behind"

  This song has the same message as the former, but concentrates more on the competition aspect of working toward goals as if it were a race. The singer is saying that he is not going to get caught up in that because having mental peace means more to him than material possessions or superficial status through others' eyes.

- "Drive" by Incubus (21)

  In the beginning he is unsure and fears what may happen, and he lets that control his life. Then he realizes that he cannot let uncertainty or fear of what may happen control his life. He decides to take control back.

  "Whatever tomorrow brings, I'll be there with open arms and open eyes"

  He has found his inner strength and taken control back, he welcomes whatever may come. He hopes it will be good, but is prepared if it's not.

  Finally, at the end of the song he sings that his life is better now because he has found that strength and has used it to take back control of his life, and through that he has found peace.

- "The Cave" by Mumford & Sons (22)

    I feel this song is a man singing to a person who has not fulfilled his goal and is now depressed, and he is telling the man to be optimistic.

    "I'll find strength in pain, and I will change my ways"

    I think this is the person replying. He is saying he will find that inner strength and stop feeling defeated, even if times are tough.

    Then later in the song he says that he wants to live his life the best way he can and how he should, which is without the bad feelings.

- Another Bob Marley song that speaks to me is "No Woman, No Cry" (23).

    "In this bright future you can't forget your past"

    It is similar to "We Are The Champions" in that it is about retrospection. Look back at the good times and the hard times. The good memories will make you happy, and the others will help you realize what you have accomplished. As I said before, just don't become stuck in them.

- The last song by Bob Marley that takes me to a better place is "Three Little Birds" (24).

    "Don't worry about a thing, 'cause every little thing gonna be all right"

    Like the other songs, this song reminds me to relax and let some worry go. It is impossible to know that "every little thing" will be all right, but it is still soothing to me. In this song he also sings of listening to birds singing and smiling because the sun is out. When I am feeling stressed I listen to the birds as well as music, and when I hear them chirping I think of these words. I am also always sure to smile with the morning sun!

- A song with the same theme as both Bob Marley songs is by Bob McFerrin and is titled "Don't Worry, Be Happy" (25). I think that almost anyone who hears this song is also taken to a better place. The island singing is relaxing, and the whistling is very pretty. The most important line in this song to me is:

    "In every life we have some trouble, but when you worry you make it double"

    Dwelling on a problem or fear very often makes it worse.

• There are songs on Eminem's latest album "Recovery" which are inspirational and I can relate to, the first being "Cinderella Man" (26) [explicit lyrics]. The overall message is the same as what I believe and have written, which is live your life to the fullest.

In the beginning he speaks of his past and the dangers he faced, but also how despite those he survived.

"It feels good, guess I'm lucky, some of us don't get a second chance"

He feels that means he is here for a purpose and he is not going to take it for granted. I feel this way too. I definitely feel like Cinderella because I could have died in my accidents, eye and car. As I wrote, I've dealt with many hard times throughout my life, but I have worked through those and come out smiling. I feel proud for doing this, even though I had to go through the hard times to find my inner strength and peace.

• The second song on the album that I can relate to is "Talkin' 2 Myself" (27) [explicit lyrics].

It reminds me of all the troubles I've had over the years, especially since my accident. It also reminds me that it is important to talk to people and get the feelings out, as I wrote in my 'journal' and 'other people' tips. When I hear this I remember I am not sad, because I know how far I have come now. I do still have sad feelings at times, and listening to this song reminds me that I need to get those feelings out and that I am not the only one with these feelings.

It is also a song of positive progression. In the beginning of the song he is upset at his situation and wants to take it out on others. He also takes those feelings out on himself. He says that he felt very bad, put himself down regularly, and it was bad for his body too. He realizes that he needs to lift himself up and start making quality music again, for himself and for his fans:

"Your health is declining with your self-esteem, you're crying out for help"

He then says that he has returned with a strong force and he will not go back to that place again. This is how I feel, and how I hope that everyone who has been to or is in a dark place feels or will feel. As I said, being sad and upset will not change anything. We all need to see the light, move towards it and never turn back.

- "Right Now" by Van Halen (28)

    This stresses the importance of starting the process of achieving your goal. With pain and fatigue, it can be very easy to just say that you will do it tomorrow. It can then be very easy for days to turn to weeks, then weeks to months, and so on. While it is important to not do too much too fast, like Alabama teaches us, it is also important to not procrastinate indefinitely.

    "Make future plans, don't dream about yesterday,
      C'mon turn, turn this thing around"

    This reiterates important messages I have given: Do not be trapped in the past, dwelling on things that cannot be changed and only make you unhappy. Turn any negativity in your life into positivity. They also say in the song "Catch that magic moment" and "It means everything." I believe both of these are true. Enjoy your life.

- "Dream On" by Aerosmith (29)

    "Dream until your dreams come true"

    This really needs no explanation. It tells us to never give up, and never stop aspiring to make our lives better and be the best person we can.

- "Best Of What's Around" by Dave Matthews Band (30)

    "Seeing things from a better side than most can dream"

    This is a song about optimism and not losing hope, much like "Don't Worry, Be Happy." The message is to do the best with what you have, and do not concentrate on what you lack.

- "Everyday" by Dave Matthews Band (31)

    "Pick me up, love, from the bottom"

    Love has the power to lift us up we were are at our worst. When we feel sad, we should look to those close to us for comfort and strength. They can fill our hearts and head with joy, and give us that lift we need to persevere and reach our goals. We should also look for that love inside to rejuvenate ourselves and start anew with vigor to aid us.

The band Metallica, who plays my favorite song "Fade to Black" (32), had an accident very similar to mine. This happened on the tour bus traveling between Stockholm and Copenhagen on September 27, 1986. It was the middle of the night, and the driver began to slide off the road. When he turned the wheel to get back on he overcorrected, just as happened in my accident. In this case, the weight of the bus caused it to fall on its side. Unfortunately, member Cliff Burton was killed in this accident. Despite this the band has not given up and is still pursuing its dreams, and I believe that is what Cliff would want. I'm sure he is still with them in spirit, just as my dad is with me.

I love this song for the beautiful music that literally gives me goosebumps every time I hear it, but also for the words and message I take from it. The subject of the song is saying that he feels empty inside and does not want to go on:

"Things not what they used to be, missing one inside of me"

These words are important to me because they remind me of how I felt at the beginning of my paralysis: my legs did not work, so I did not work. I remember thinking about (and doing) the extra amount of effort just to do the same tasks, and crying. I cried because I was frustrated, and because I knew that I was going to have to keep exerting that much more energy to do those things for the rest of my life. I remember hurting and feeling very empty inside because I had lost most of my friends and was not making any new ones. In all I was completely drained and could not see the light at the end of the tunnel.

Then, I decided to turn it around because I wanted to be happy and I knew it was not "too late." I decided to live my life the best I possibly could, and have done so ever since. Now when I listen to this song I love it of course for the music that is amazing, but also to remind myself what a good choice I made. I know that I will never say those words, no matter what!

<u>What I take from all these songs</u>:

- You can do it

- It is not too late

- Do not ever give up

- Live all life to the fullest

- Also do not ever lose hope

- Be an optimist, not a pessimist

- Don't ever get stuck in unhappiness

- Every little thing is going to be all right

- Remember your abilities and achievements

- Do all you can to make your wishes come true

- Welcome the good times, and do not fear the bad

- Let go of the bad feelings, celebrate and live your life

- Look back at hard times to realize how far you have come

- Find your inner strength whether it's through struggles or not

- No matter how hard times may get know that you're never alone

What is worth the prize is always worth the fight

Achieve, live without fears

Celebrate, live without tears

My Mother

The Power of Love!

My mom is my best friend. We speak every day, on the phone or through text and email. We talk to each other about our days, but I also call her when I need help with something or when I think I have something that will make her smile. How she has dealt with all the crises in her life shows why I love and admire her so much. She was my caregiver after my trials as a child, including my car accident. Her hope and determination inspired me very much in my rehabilitation and helped me through all the work I had to do. She helped me practice all the things that I would need to be able to do to lead as normal a life as possible. All of these were very difficult in the beginning, but she would not give up or let me. With time and effort, I found that these activities did become faster and easier.

I am very thankful to her for all the help she gave me, which brings me to another 'ation,' appreciation. A large part of getting all you can out of life is being thankful for what you have, and a large part of being thankful is expressing it. I am sure to always say thank you to anyone who helps me in any way. I know that whenever I am thanked for something, I appreciate that person for thanking me. This is a win-win situation because it makes both of us feel good. This is also true of compliments. It only takes a second to tell someone you like what they are wearing or compliment them about anything else, but what you have said will most probably stay with them.

Along with appreciation is yet another 'Ation' that I feel for my mother: 'admiration.' As I said above, she has been through hard times and not "lost her cool" or broken down in the face of them. The song that I believe best expresses both of these feelings of mine for her is "Praise You" by Fatboy Slim (33). I feel that this song definitely applies to us. I am sure that it also applies to others, so I have included it. It speaks to sticking together through thick and thin, and appreciating those with whom you do that. The line that most speaks to me:

"I have to celebrate you baby, I have to praise you like I should"

These words express my feelings very well. It is important to make people aware of any gratitude you feel toward them. These feelings can be expressed in many ways, from a simple "thank you" to a gift.

I thought about this, and it led me to write this free-verse poem for her. I wrote the first four stanzas and gave it to her for Mother's Day 2008. I then added the last five and gave that to her in 2010:

For My Mother

You are everything that I strive to be

You are intelligent,

Thoughtful,

And above all,

Cool

The way in which you deal with trying

Situations in a non-catastrophic

Manner speaks to your

Perseverance and strength as

A person

You are truly the best role model

That I could ask for

The fact that you could weather all the

Hurdles that have stood in your way

Without breaking down

Is a testament to your good attitude

You have always been my rock during

The times when my life has been

A tumultuous sea

I hope to follow your example

And do the same for others and

For you should you ever need it,

But I also hope that you never do

It is hard to find the words to express the

Depth of my love for you and for

The bond we share

Thank you for setting an example

And being a person

That I am proud to aspire

To be like

Remember, we are simply being thrown

Curveballs to perfect our swings

She was very touched by this, as I hoped she would be. She now has
it displayed in her house where she or any visitors can look at or read anytime.

This is a note I wrote for my mom for Mother's Day 2004. She laminated it, and it is still on her refrigerator door:

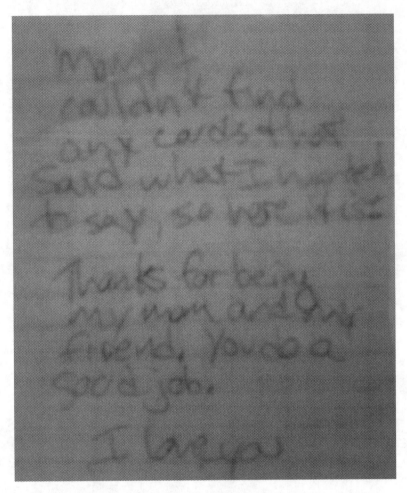

"Mom, I couldn't find any cards that said
what I wanted to say, so here it is:

"Thanks for being my mom and my friend.
You do a good job.

"I love you"

My Father
Love From the Other Side

  As well as looking inside ourselves to find joy and reassurance, we can (and should) look to others for it. As I said in my sundae section, my dad passed away in 2009. I miss him very much. I do believe that there is an afterlife and that he is still watching over the people he cares about and helping us whenever he can. I know there have been times since his passing that I needed to know he was with me, and he has shown me he was and always will be.

  Next is the cover of my dad's funeral card, and I like the title very much. I also love the picture of him on the cover. He is comfortable and relaxed, just enjoying life. After that is the story of his life, and the description of his personality and who he was, written by my aunt. She captured it quite nicely:

A Celebration of Life

Robert E. Pabst

September 19, 1954 – August 13, 2009

Robert Edmond Pabst (Bobby) was the first born to Ron and Betty Pabst on September 19, 1954, in Ft. Campbell, Kentucky. The family moved to Indianapolis in 1956 and they eventually made Zionsville their home. Bobby grew up with three younger siblings: Judy Rabourn, Richard and Ronnie Pabst. He graduated from Zionsville High School in 1972. After graduation he attended Indiana Mechanical School and received his journeyman certification. Following graduation he began working for the family business, Ron Pabst Plumbing, where he worked throughout his career.

Bobby met Lisa Clevenger from Richmond, Indiana and she became the love of his life, marrying on November 20, 1982. The second love of his life, their daughter Jessica Leigh Pabst, was born on June 15, 1983. Bob, Lisa and Jess made Zionsville their home for the next twenty-six years. His pride and joy Jess recently graduated from IUPUI with a degree in Spanish Education.

His favorite pastimes were gardening, fishing and car racing. He was a friend to all whom he met and was always ready to lend a helping hand. He had a love for Rock & Roll music and always enjoyed a good time with his lifelong friends.

Bob's humor and his natural zest for life will be sadly missed by his family and all whom had the great fortune to have known him."

Written by Reasa Pabst

73

No one is ever truly gone if they are not forgotten. Celebrate the person and what they brought into your life, as well as letting them live on through yourself and your actions. There is a song, also by Eminem, which applies to this topic: "You're Never Over" (34). In this he is talking about his best friend that died in 2006. He says:

"You may be gone, but you're never over"

In this song he also says he doesn't think his friend understood how much he meant to him. This relates to my "–Ation" of appreciation. Voice your feelings towards the people you love and treasure. Make sure they know what they mean to you and what they bring into your life. This, along with the expression of compliments I wrote about, will lift many hearts and create many smiles.

The signs I get from my father are mainly through music. I can turn on the radio and say: "Dad show me," and most always the next song that comes on is one of my favorites or one that makes me think of him. Dad and I used to listen to many songs and dance in the living room while I was growing up, but if I had to name one song that was "our song" it would definitely be The Rolling Stones' "Miss You" (35). This is one of my five favorite songs of all time. I still remember dancing with him in the living room to that song. I inherited from him what we call the 'Pabst lips.' They are very full, and fun to show off.

Our favorite line is right in the middle of the song: "What's the matter with you boy?" When that line would play, my dad would crouch down so that he was at my level. Then we would point at each other and sing it. While we were singing this together, we would make sure we showed off the big lips when doing to "W" and "B" sounds. As I say at the end of the book, one of my dreams is to meet the band and sing that with Mick like dad and I used to do!

We always had fun when that song was playing, but also during others. The musical artists that always remind me of him:

- The Rolling Stones
- The Allman Brothers Band
- Eric Clapton
- The Beatles
- The Grateful Dead

- John Hiatt
- B.B. King
- Little Feat
- John Prine
- Van Morrison

I know that music is the way he communicates with me from the other side because he and I love it so much. As I said, I have always kept a journal where I write down experiences that are interesting, funny and heartwarming so that I will always be able to look back and remember.

Here are some of the times I know were communications from my dad:

#1

I was listening to the radio. When the song I was listening to ended, the station went to a commercial. I went over to the radio and changed the station. As I was changing, I asked my dad to show me through the music that he was still watching over me. When I got to my other favorite station, the song that was playing was The Allman Brothers Band's "Jessica" (36). This is another of my five favorite songs, for the reason that is obvious and for the beautiful music. The song was at the very beginning so I was able to listen to all of it.

I was so moved by this that I was crying, but it was a happy cry. When the song ended, I asked my dad to "do it again." Then the next song that came on was "Layla" by Derek and The Dominos (37). This is in my top ten favorite songs. We used to dance to it in the living room too. I listened, danced, and cried more tears of love, joy, and appreciation. When the song was over I changed the radio back to the first station. As I was pressing the back button, I was saying in my head that the only possible thing that could make the experience any better would be if a certain song was playing on the station once I got to it.

My dad must have heard my thoughts, because when I reached the station it was indeed playing the song "Free Bird" by Lynyrd Skynyrd (38). I call it "my second favorite song of all time ever" (after "Fade to Black") to express the emphasis. I love it for the beautiful music, as well as the lyrics I feel apply to me and many others who listen to it. It was the main reason I had been listening to my Lynyrd Skynyrd CD earlier that day. It has been one of my favorite songs since my early teenage years, but the accident and the paralysis have made me perceive it in a different way.

The song is a man telling his mate that he is now free and will not change his ways, and if she does not like that she should go. I have always concentrated on the freedom aspect of the song. When I was younger, it was freedom from "authority figures" and school. I think that all teenagers experience this at some point while growing up. As I aged, and after my car accident, these lyrics took on a new meaning: now the freedom I wanted was from my injuries, pain and bad feelings.

When I hear this song I dance (as I said before) with my eyes closed, fully taking in the beauty of the music. I knew hearing that song was the only way that the experience as a whole could possibly be any better than it already was, and my dad knew it too!

My loving father holding me. Not very flattering to me. Ha-ha!

#2

One morning I was in bed trying to decide whether I wanted to get up and start my day, or sleep in a little more. I knew I should get up, but I was still sleepy. I decided to just turn on the radio and listen for a little while. When I did there was a song playing that wasn't one of my favorites, but something made me leave it on that station and listen to the rest of it. The song ended about one minute later, and then the next one came on. Sure enough, that song was "Miss You." This woke me and I quickly got out of bed and into my chair so I could dance.

I was also trying to hear his voice, but I could not remember what it sounded like. I asked him to please let me hear it again. I waited, and then I just heard him in my head say "Jej." This was his nickname for me my whole life. My full name is Jessica Leigh Pabst. When I was first learning to talk and people would ask me what my name was, I would tell them "Jeja Leigh." Dad shortened this to Jej, and called me by that name my whole life. When I heard this in my head I was very happy.

Then I thought that he should give me another sign to confirm that playing the song really was from him. Then I changed my mind because I **knew** it was from him. When that song ended, the next song that came on was The Black Crowes' "She Talks to Angels" (39). One of the chorus lines in that song is "They call her out by her name." This gave me comfort chills and told me that even though I didn't need a confirmation sign, he still gave me one. He was telling me that he was the angel I was talking to and who said my name. I thanked him again, and went on with a smile on my face.

#3

I was listening to the radio. The song ended, so I changed the station. As I was, I asked my dad to please show me he was with me. When I got to the station I wanted, I just sat back and listened. It was the **very beginning** of "Jessica." I was filled with joy and comfort.

What really made me laugh was that I had been listening to that song on The Allman Brothers Band's Greatest Hits CD earlier that day, but I stopped so that I could listen to something different. When "Jessica" ended, I said to myself "Well I guess he was not done listening to them," and smiled.

Then I asked him to please play for me another one of our songs to show me that it was not just a coincidence. When the next song started, it was "Layla." Again, I sat back and enjoyed. When that song ended, I changed the radio back to the first station I had been listening to.

While doing this, I was thinking that there was only one song that could make this joyfully overwhelming experience any better: "Free Bird" (of course). When I reached the station I wanted,

Guess what was playing?!?!?!

This question fills a whole page of my journal. Under the question I wrote: "Dad, I know you are still with me and with Mom. Thank you." Then, under that line I wrote: "I love you," also very large in red ink.

Luck?

I was playing a dice game with a couple friends. I have listed all details of the game so anyone reading can then play the game if they would like.

Rules:

- In the game fives are fifty points each and ones are one hundred points each.

- Three of the same number is that number times one hundred, except ones (three of those are one thousand points).

- The only possible score higher than three ones is to get a straight (1, 2, 3, 4, 5, 6). The score of this roll is fifteen hundred points, and is extremely rare.

- The other bonus to this roll is that if you want to roll all the dice again you can.

- The player can keep rolling as long as they are getting points. However, if they roll and do not get any points, they have to stop rolling and they lose all the points of that roll.

- The first player to reach ten thousand points wins the game.

While I was playing, I was thinking of my dad. We used to play it as a family on Friday nights, or if there were already many people I would sit on my dad's lap and play.

In my head I asked him to help me. I even said out loud "Come on Dad!" On my next roll I got a straight, and even though it was risky I chose to roll them all again. That time I rolled three ones and a five. That meant that my score on the roll as a whole was 2,550 points! Then because of that roll, and my dad I believe, I won the game. It just made me feel good to think that he was with me, and was helping me out!

Funny Dad

At my mom's office Christmas party

I believe my dad has also communicated through the internet. One day I was at my mom's house washing dishes. We had eaten pizza the night before, and instead of a slicer she used her ceramic knife to cut the pizza because it was sharper. I was cleaning that knife, and accidentally cut myself. It was even so bad that I had to go to the Immediate Care.

The next morning I checked my emails, and one of those was an advertisement for that very same knife. I really believe that was him messing with me, trying to cheer me up when I was upset. It is too ironic to be just a coincidence, and I think he knew it would make me smile.

Aunt Kate

I am not the only one who has experienced these signs from my dad. My mother's sister Kate has also had an experience in which she believes my dad had a part, and it was also through music. After he had been gone for a week and a half, she was listening to Little Feat's "Waiting for Columbus" CD. She told me that she calls this her "Bobby CD" because it always reminds her of him.

She went outside and as she came back in she heard that the music was skipping. The CD was stuck and just kept repeating one line over and over again. The song was "Mercenary Territory" (40) and the line was "I'd do it all over again." She said that the CD had never skipped before, and because of this she believes it was a message from my dad. She believes it was him saying that he was happy with his life and if he had it to do all again, he would. She told me that she had real peace with that.

"Uncle" Steve

My dad's best friend, who is like an uncle to me, has also gotten signs. They first met in the mid 1970s when they were both in their early twenties. They were roommates and traveled together for a while, and remained friends after they were done living together.

Steve told me that one evening about two months after my dad had passed away, he was "snoozing" on his couch when his roommate Dave woke him. When he opened his eyes he saw that the pole lamp in the corner of the room had fallen over. It luckily was close enough to the corner that it did not completely fall over and break, but it was clear that it had been knocked over by someone or something.

Dave asked Steve why he'd done that, and he told him that he hadn't. Steve told me that he suspected it could have been a sign from my dad because he had just been talking with Dave about Dad earlier that day, but he didn't let himself get carried away with that thought.

Then later that night, Dave and Steve were watching television when a cup sitting on the coffee table fell over. Steve said: "That's weird." Then Dave asked "You didn't do that?", and Steve replied that he hadn't. Then when he got up to clean the table off, the t.v. began changing channels. The television remote control was on a different table, so neither of the men were near it.

Usually, when Steve changed the channel on his television the screen would be black for a second, and then it would show the picture of the new channel. However, he told me that this time there were no black screens when the channel changed. He said that it would simply go from the picture of one channel directly in to the picture of the next.

Dave then looked at the memorial card for my dad that was handed out at his funeral and told Steve that he believed it was him "messing" with them from the other side because they had just been talking about him. Steve agreed, and I do too.

Steve told me that the experience as a whole did not scare him, but instead comforted him and brought him joy to know "Bobby" was still with him. This is also true of all the experiences I have had. I also hope that if others begin to look for these signs and do recognize that they are getting them, it will bring them comfort and joy also.

My best experience

I was out with my friend and we went to an Indianapolis Colts game. I was wearing my Colts sweatshirt and my friend was wearing my dad's old Colts sweatshirt. The Colts won the game, and I attributed this in part to my dad. It is just pleasing to think that he had a part in it, like I do with my Packers.

After the game we were in the car driving home and listening to the car radio when one of my favorite songs, "(Don't Fear) The Reaper" by Blue Oyster Cult (41), came on the radio. The strange part about this is that the shirt I was wearing under the sweatshirt had a quote on it from the Saturday Night Live skit involving that song.

The skit is the band in the studio recording that song for release. They are in the sound booth doing takes and Christopher Walken, playing their manager, is listening. He stops them and comes into the booth to say that they should play more of the cowbell in the song. They try again, but he comes into the booth with them and says he wants more. The most humorous line of that skit is when he comes back in the second time and says: "I've got a fever, and the only prescription is more cowbell!" (42). I was wearing that shirt because all of my Colts T-shirts were still in storage from the fire, and it was the only blue (the shirt) and white (the writing) clothing I had (the Colts' colors).

I believed this was my dad communicating with me through music again to show me that he was with me, so I thanked him out loud. Then the music stopped. It was silent for around ten seconds, then came back on. I told my friend that this was from my dad and I was happy he had done it. After that I sarcastically said: "Thanks dad, another experience to write about in my book." Right then, the music stopped again. This time it was only silent for around five seconds, but it was still awesome (figuratively and literally!).

I would have been happy with only those signs, but there were more. I had asked my friend earlier that day what his favorite song was and he told me "Dream On" by Aerosmith. That was the song that played when "The Reaper" was over. I told him that my dad must have been listening when he had told me that earlier. I sang along, despite being stunned. When the song was over the station went to a commercial. I changed to a different station while saying out loud "Come on Dad, do it again."

When I got to the other rock and roll station, they were playing the very beginning of "Free Bird." This stunned me. I was almost breathless. My mouth was wide open, and all I could do was point at the radio with one hand and clench the other in a fist over my heart. I did not cry this time like I did the others, partly because I was too overwhelmed, but mostly because I felt such a feeling of comfort. I just sang along and thought about my dad, and how happy I was that my friend was there to witness all of it.

Now it is true that all of these could have just been coincidences, but I know in my heart they were not. I wanted to share them because I know how much comfort and joy they have brought me, and I hope to spread those feelings. I hope the people who read this will look for signs and will discover that someone they thought that they had lost is still with them in some form.

Although we should remember that those people are still with us, we should not be overwhelmed and let the sadness take over. I believe the poem on my father's memorial card, "Miss Me, But Let Me Go"(43) by Amy Louise Kerswell, says how we should treat this perfectly. It is person who is gone speaking. They are saying to simply remember the good times you shared. The big message is to not be sorrowful at the passing of someone you care about, because they have simply moved on to the next step in their journey. The restates my message of not being sad about something you cannot change because there is no point:

"Miss me a little, but not too long,

And not with your head bowed low,

Remember the love that we once shared,

Miss me, but let me go"

<u>Purpose</u>
Why I have shared this

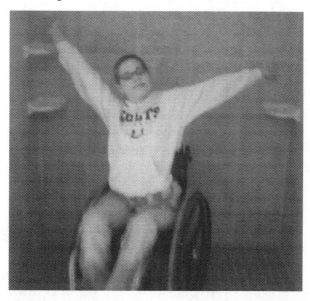

My new shower in my remodeled bathroom

I am not writing for pity or for sorrow. The purpose of my writing is to help and to show that I have things I want to accomplish in life and I am not going to let paralysis, pain, a brain injury, epilepsy, the loss of my father and pets I loved, a house fire or anything else stop me. While I know all situations are different, I believe no one should let anything stop them from living the life they want. It is important to look inside yourself and to the people close to you, living and passed, for strength in accomplishing your goals and getting all that you can from life, while also enjoying it.

There are things that I cannot do anymore because of my paralysis, and that hurts me. There are also things that I can still do, but are much more complicated. It is so frustrating at times I want to cry and scream at the same time. At times I still do cry, even after twelve years. When things get this bad I often ask out loud "Why?". I am just trying to live my life and things should not be so difficult. I do not try to cover up these feelings or ignore them, but I also do not let them take over. I rise above the anger and sadness because they will only make it worse.

As I said before, one thing that has helped me to deal with the hard times over the last decade is appreciation for what I do have. I believe that is the key to happiness. We appreciate all things that make us feel good inside. Most of all we appreciate those around us, both for what they bring in to our lives and for what they allow us to bring in to theirs. I know that the people around me bring me much joy, so I let them know this and try my best to bring them the same amount of joy.

I am sure to recognize all the good things in my life and cherish them as much as I can. When times are tough, thinking of those things helps me. I also remember that there are many people living in circumstances much worse than mine. I am not trying to negate my feelings, I just think it is important to keep perspective. It is not fair that some have to do so much more just to live a normal life, but doing so while not breaking down is an awesome feat.

Again, the most important thing that I remember when I am sad or upset is that it won't solve anything. Being mad or sad will not reverse what happened, so there is no point. When I remember that, I let those negative feeling go and bring in the positive. My goal in life is to help people and bring smiles to their faces. I hope that this book has helped me to accomplish that in some part.

As I am sure you can tell by now, I do not believe in unhappiness. I know that it exists, but I think that the less attention we give it the less power it has over us. Once again, my ultimate view:

It is much better to live With a smile on your Face than tears!

Overcoming

While Metallica's "Fade to Black" is my favorite song and all the songs I have listed inspire me to stay positive and move forward, I believe the song which best applies to me and to anyone that has been through hard times is not any of those. That honor, for me at least, goes to Mr. Johnny Nash and his song "I Can See Clearly Now" (44). This song perfectly voices how I feel and how I hope my book can help others feel.

He sings that he has now moved past the unhappiness that had prevented him from living the way he wanted:

"Gone are the dark clouds that had me blind"

He made his peace, decided not to let the sadness take over his life, and has now come out of it smiling. He does recognize that there may be other difficulties in the future, but he knows he will be able to deal with those and happily move on.

As I said before, I am a fan of the rapper Eminem. I know he speaks from his heart, and the way he puts words together in rhyme is very impressive. While his songs have some explicit lyrics and I have not been in the same situations he rhymes about, I feel I can definitely relate to many of the messages his songs carry. I have already written about the songs "Cinderella Man," "Talkin' 2 Myself," and "You're Never Over" from his new album. Along with these, there another song that I feel a strong connection with: "Not Afraid" (45) [explicit lyrics]. In this song he speaks of dealing with issues, as Mr. Nash did in his.

He says he is tired of the way he had been living, which was not confronting problems, and is going to change that:

"I'm standing up, I'ma face my demons"

He invites other people to join him in the journey and confront their own problems. Things like this can be very hard to do alone, but having friends to support you can ease that and increase confidence very much. In addition to backing you up it is also great to have friends to celebrate achievements with, be they yours or theirs. We all know the joy of accomplishment, so we like to show those feelings to others as much as receiving them ourselves.

In the song he says to tell him your story if you have also experienced that, so here's mine:

Although mine was a different type of rehabilitation, I feel like I have been down that road. Actually, I feel I lived on it for a while! However, I worked through it and I did not let it get me down. I did not, and will not, let my misfortunes force me to live my life in a cage. I do not fear what 'may' happen, or dwell on what has happened in the past. Those were my demons, that I faced and against whom I held my ground. I will do my best to share my knowledge and bring people together so no one has to deal with the changes or go through this often scary process alone in the future. I will not let anything stop me from being happy and living my life the way I want, or stop me from helping others to do the same. And if that is the only way I am able to stand, that is okay with me.

There is one of Vince Lombardi's quote that means more to me than any of the previous. It is my life motto and the one that I hope means the most to my readers. I hope it will inspire you just as it has me:

"It's not whether you get knocked down, it's whether you get up"[46]

Messages

Think about and remember:

- Recognize the good & do not concentrate on the bad.

- Hope for the best, but also prepare for the worst.

- Tough times never last. Tough people do.

- Everyone enjoys hearing kind words.

- Treat every single day as a gift.

- Treasure all that you have.

- Achieving goals may take time.

- Don't live in chains, you have the key.

- What does not kill you makes you stronger.

- No one is ever truly gone if they are not forgotten.

- Do not dwell on what is lost. Appreciate what remains.

Let go of bad feelings. Celebrate and live your life.

Life goes on!

It has been twelve years for me now, And I am still kickin'!

Well
Not Kickin',
But You
Know What
I Mean!

Vase of Appreciation

I am thankful I am alive when I could be dead

Tears will change nothing, I smile instead

It is from our past experiences we learn

Also from those comes the strength we earn

I treasure all that I have, possessions and love

As well as a spirit that I am proud of

I believe I have now found my mission in life

To help those whose worlds now seem filled with strife

I will help them and pass on the things I have learned

And hope then some ease in their lives will return

Through this there will then come a new dawn

And the feelings of sadness will be gone

Once again, I am thankful that I am alive

Difficulties may come, but I'll take them in stride

Jessica Pabst, 2011

"Never underestimate the powers of the handicapped!"

–Damon Wayans as "Handi–Man" on In Living Color

IN ALL

- Recognize the good & do not concentrate on the bad.
- Hope for the best but also prepare for the worst.
- Tough times never last. Tough people do.
- Everyone enjoys hearing kind words.
- Treat every single day as a gift.
- Treasure all that you have.
- Every good thing may take time.
- Don't live in chains. You have the key.
- What does not kill you makes you stronger.
- No one is ever truly gone if they're not forgotten.
- Don't dwell on what is lost. Appreciate what remains.
- You can do it
- It is not too late
- Do not ever give up
- Live all life to the fullest
- Also do not ever lose hope
- Be an optimist, not a pessimist
- Don't ever get stuck in unhappiness
- Every little thing is going to be all right
- Remember your abilities and achievements
- Do all you can to make your wishes come true
- Welcome the good times, and do not fear the bad
- Let go of the bad feelings, celebrate and live your life
- Look back at hard times to realize how far you have come
- Find your inner strength whether it's through struggles or not
- No matter how hard times may get know that you're never alone

What is worth the prize is always worth the fight

Achieve, live without fears. Celebrate, live without tears!

Words of Two Great Thinkers

"*Your time is limited,*
"*Have the courage to follow your heart and intuition.*
"*They somehow already know*
"*What you truly want to become.*"

-Steve Jobs,
From the 2005 Stanford Commencement Address (47)

Excerpt of "Life" by Mother Teresa (48)

Life is an opportunity, benefit from it.

Life is a dream, realize it.

Life is too precious, do not destroy it.

Life is life, fight for it.

Post Notes

Finding answers and comfort

Coming to terms and adjusting to a life with paralysis can be a very scary and difficult process. As I said, that is the main reason I have written this book. Beside my and other books, there are many places where people can find answers to the questions they have and find comfort through sharing feelings and talking with others. As I said, many hospitals and rehabilitation clinics have weekly meetings for this purpose. There are also other ways if those do not work for you. One that I was introduced to and like very much is www.Inspire.com (50). This is a paralysis resource center support community website. It connects patients and those around them to others that can offer advice and support.

The company is based in New Jersey, but the website allows people from all over the world to join. The information page of the site states it was created because:

- "We all need a safe place to discuss health.
- "We can help each other.
- "Together, we are better."

The website allows its members to make friends with similar interests, learn about conditions important to them, post journal entries and any questions they might have, and respond to any other member's questions they feel they can answer or at least weigh in on.

The website also allows members to search keywords to find any existing posts about a topic important to them. As of today there are 267,192 members and 42,666,769 posts, but these grow every day. When someone joins, they make a profile with information about themselves. This includes a basic description (age, sex, location), but also one that is more in-depth (why the person has chosen to join the group, their interests and their outlook on life).

There is an option on the profile page to receive post notifications to your regular email address. This will let you know when any new questions are posted, and any replies to those questions. Next is an example of a post with some basic questions one of the members asked, and my responses to those. I am not an expert, but I told her what I believe to be true and what I felt would help answer her questions and make her feel better:

She wanted to know why she could still feel pain, even though she was paralyzed. She said she felt the pain up in the areas she should not have, and didn't understand why that was. For instance, it should have been her lower back hurting, but she felt it in her upper back and arms. She did not think this was fair, and many other people do not either.

Her second question was about "going to the bathroom." She did not have feeling low enough to know when she was "going," but every time she does she gets goosebumps and her body hair stands up, and wanted to know why.

Her final question was about sensation below her injury level, which was T3. This is a little lower than the top of the shoulders, but she said she could feel lower than that (deep rubs, not light touching). She asked if this was good and if it meant she was healing.

My responses to these:

"I believe you still feel pain and rubbing because your spinal cord is not severed. It's just damaged. Mine is the same: just a little torn up. I even have a couple places on my legs where when I touch them it is just like touching my arm. Some feeling still gets through, but big messages and signals such as telling the leg to move cannot. That means that the body signals like pain or needing to go to the bathroom also have trouble getting through.

"The bad thing about pain is that it radiates. The pain is coming from that hurt area, but moving to where you can feel. If you cut your finger, your whole hand and arm also hurt. We just don't notice that extra pain because the finger hurts so bad. If your finger went numb after hurting it, then you would feel that pain in your arm.

"As far as the goosebumps and stuff, it is the body reacting to sensations. The body always knows when you have to 'use the bathroom,' so it tells you. Before the paralysis you could feel that and didn't need any extra signals. Now that your spinal cord is damaged the body reacts in a different way to sensations. I think there are some people without spinal cord damage that get goosebumps too. You just get them more intensely because the spinal cord damage has magnified that feeling.

"Not to upset you, but like I said: I have had this feeling since my accident almost 13 years ago, and I am still not able to move my legs. The feeling is still a blessing though. I love my lower half tingling all the time. I love that it reacts if I hurt it. I can feel if my toes are bunched in my shoes or something, and my legs will jump if they feel pain. You should move them as much as you can because it will strengthen those muscles and may bring back more movement ability.

"The other positive of having only spinal cord damage is that stem cell surgery is promising. In super layperson's terms: Stem cells are mimics. They become whatever cells they are around. So if a doctor were to put some on the spinal cord, they would become those cells and heal it. I know it is much more complicated, but that is the basic idea as I understand it.

"I know people on this website have had that surgery and it has been successful. It's just hard for many people to get it because it requires leaving the country and going to where it is not illegal. I do not understand why the president and congress don't reverse the law. It is true one of the places you can get them is from aborted babies, but there are others. Placentas also contain them. I am not worried about time though. I will just wait patiently because I don't hate, or even dislike, my life."

The are other helpful websites with support groups like this one, and there are also meetings that can be attended in person. I know there are some my area, so I am sure there are also in your area. These are often held at rehabilitation centers one or two nights a week.

Compassion

An issue I have strong feelings about is compassion. I hope I have shown through this book that I believe it is wrong to make assumptions and judge on appearance alone, or even before you truly know a person. There is a song that illustrates this feeling well, and that is "What It's Like" by Everlast (51) [explicit lyrics]. He sings of three main situations that are difficult for the people in them. He conveys the feelings of the people in those situations, and how people react to them. This leads us to imagine how we would feel if we were those people in the same situations. This one of those three is a man that has lost his job and is living on the street begging for change:

"God forbid you ever had to walk a mile in his shoes"

Think of these things before judging. All circumstances are different.

Dad

1) I was out with my friend and was telling her how happy I was with finishing my book, and that all I had left to do was edit it (funny wordplay–say it out loud: "edit it"). Then when I get done I can say that I edited it (say that out loud: "edited it". Ha-ha-ha!). I just had to find a publisher that would take a chance on me and it would hopefully be smooth sailing after that.

I told her that I had the brief bio, para–tips, para–perks, bathroom activities and jokes in the main section of the book. Then I told her that I also had a Mom section and a Dad section. The Mom section being what she means to me and the way we have gotten through all the hard times together, and the Dad section telling ways he has spoken to me from the other side.

Then, I asked my dad to show me he was with me. The next song that came on was one that I have listed as inspirational, "Trenchtown Rock." When that song ended, I asked him to show me again. The next song? "Already Gone" by The Eagles. The song that played after those two? "Sweet Child O' Mine" by Guns N' Roses (52). This did make me cry. These were also not sad tears. They were tears of comfort and love because I knew it was my dad with me.

After my friend dropped me off at home, I asked my dad to give me one last sign that it was him doing all of that. Then I had to call my doctor's office, and they put me on hold while they were getting my chart. The song that was playing on the hold music? "Every Breath You Take (I'll Be Watching You)" by Sting and the Police (53). I was breathless again.

2) I was listening to a local radio show one morning. They were playing songs from the past and seeing how quickly the guests could name the artist and song.

They started playing a song, but the guest did not know so they gave a hint: "He has the same name as a beer." The guest then knew and said: "Steve Miller Band." The host said: "You're right," but someone in the background said: "It's Bob Pabst." There are no words for that, except 'awesome.'

As I said, I hope that everyone who reads this and has lost someone close to them will start looking for these signs if they believe it could bring them comfort. I know it has made me feel much better to know that he is not truly gone.

Mini-Bed Buddy

In the story and trials sections, I mentioned my stuffed animal penguin Opus that I had gotten after my eye injury but lost in the fire. For Christmas 2011 my mom gave me another one. She said it was very hard to find because it has been so many years since those comics were out. The "Outland" comic ended in 1995. Then in 2003 the character got his own comic "Opus," but that ended in 2008.

When I opened the box and saw him, I started crying. They were tears of surprise and joy. This Opus is smaller than my old one, but that is good. I now sleep with him on top of the pillow in front of me at night. Again, this gives me extra help to hold my shoulder up straight.

One Last Piece of Advice

A member of the Inspire website posted a complaint about the word "disabled." He said that it applied to so many people for so many different reasons that it was essentially meaningless, and this angered him. He said that he was very active and so he felt the term being applied to him was derogatory and he was offended. He felt that people automatically make assumptions when using this word to describe someone, no matter the abilities of the individual.

My response:

"You should not let things like this get to you so much. It is a term that people feel is politically correct and broad enough to cover many people whose abilities are not the same, or impaired, for any number of reasons.

"I do not believe this term will go away, even with protests from people that it may apply to. Therefore, being worked up or angry about it will only perhaps give you a stress ulcer or affect your health in some other unfortunate way. This is an example of something we must rise above..."

When filling out your profile on the Inspire website, you are able to tell your inspiration. Mine:

"It comes from many places. What I want to accomplish, as well as what I already have. All those around me, as well as what is inside me. Finally, the dreams I have, as well as the realities I know."

One Last Lombardi Quote (similar to former)

"The greatest accomplishment is not in never falling,
But in rising again after you fall."(54)

One Last Dose

I recently heard another song I was able to change a little to make it "funny." That song is "Paradise" by Coldplay (55). The song is about a girl dreaming of a better life, and Chris Martin sings: "She'd dream of Para-para-paradise, Para-para-paradise, Para-para-paradise."

When I heard this I immediately thought: "I'm Para-para-paralyzed, Para-para-paralyzed, Para-para-paralyzed."

I have included this song on my list for the humor, but also for the beautiful music and for what I have said about having and achieving dreams.

Inspiring & Humorous

There is another song that I enjoy very much. It speaks of keeping on (and keeping cool) in the face of adversity, while making listeners smile. That song is Joe Walsh's "Life's Been Good" (56). Joe sings of his misfortunes, but also that he believes: "life's been good" to him so far. People can take it as him being sarcastic but I choose to take it as him not letting bad occurrences destroy him, much the same as is my message through this book. Granted, some of the misfortunes in the song are self-inflicted and I do not condone them. However, I still do like it for the message and for the humor.

The line I can best relate to, and even echo:

"Lucky I'm sane after all I've been through"

Perfect Song

I have included many songs in my book that I believe can lift spirits and inspire my readers to reach their goals. Since I began the book, a song has come out that perfectly puts into words my purpose and goal. That song is by Phillip Phillips, and is titled "Home"(57).

It encourages people to stick together and persevere, despite any reluctancies or troubles they may have. He sings to also not give in to any fears or bad feelings that they have or may occur in the process of making their lives better and adjusting to any new circumstances.

The song reminds us to not give up when paths we take, or are forced to take, may seem difficult or even impossible. As I have said, it is not a bad thing to be sad or scared. It is only a bad thing to get lost in those feelings and lose all hope. My favorite line in the song is also the most appropriate for my book. In it Phillips tells his listeners to not feel isolated or scared in the new situation. He sings:

"Just know you're not alone, cause I'm going to make this place your home"

By this I mean make you comfortable where you are in your life now. Don't pay attention to the voices that may be telling you things are impossible and your life is over. Just stay calm and know that you have the power to take back control. No matter how hard things may seem and how isolated you may feel, they are not impossible and you are not alone.

What makes this song even more personal is when speaking of traveling down this road to a better future, the word he uses "roll" instead of "walk!"

I have said these many times, but I will again one last time:

You are not alone, and you can do it!

It is never too late to enjoy your life!

Bike Rides

1) Bikes as far as the eye could see!
2) With my man Mitch (Governor Daniels).
3) All the pretty motorcycles.

These and the cover picture were taken at the Governor's charity motorcycle ride, right before we hit the road. My friend Mark rented a Harley trike (3 wheels) to take me. This is much easier than a motorcycle because the back end has two wheels instead of one. With this there is no worry of falling or needing to balance, and there are footplates so legs don't dangle. These can be seen below in the pictures from a different ride.

1) Cruisin'!!
2) Had to go show Mom!
3) Being silly at my house before we left. Pretty Harley tank top!

These are from the first time we rented the trike. It was also for a charity ride. As you can see, it was warmer then. The best thing about this ride was that we led it. We were the head of the pack. The footplate can be seen all three pictures, but in the third picture you can also see my "leg straps." I wrapped them around my legs for extra security and peace of mind.

Another advantage of the trike is the seating. This can be seen in the middle and last pictures. The back of the seat is big and wraps around. This is very comfortable and secure. I was not scared at any time on either ride. Sometimes it is very nice to feel the freedom of moving, but not being in your chair. Of course you have this in your car, but it is different and I think better on the motorcycle or any type of open vehicle.

Rebuilding a House (Before & After)

(Kitty in the window)

Rock-climbing

Black Beauty

Joy of Life

Yes, that is a "New Kids on the Block" t-shirt. Donnie "Bad Boy" Wahlberg was my favorite. And yes, I am a natural rock star, Harley chick, animal-lover and all-around goofball. I of course love the picture with my dad and uncle, but the bathtub is the best!

Songs

Inspirational/Feel Good

"I'm In A Hurry"	Alabama
"Dream On"	Aerosmith
"Trenchtown Rock"	Bob Marley
"No Woman, No Cry"	Bob Marley & The Wailers
"Three Little Birds"	Bob Marley & The Wailers
"Don't Worry, Be Happy"	Bob McFerrin
"Peace Of Mind"	Boston
"Tubthumping" (58)*	Chumbawamba
"Best Of What's Around"	Dave Matthews Band
"Everyday"	Dave Matthews Band
"Already Gone"	Eagles
"Cinderella Man"	Eminem
"Not Afraid"	Eminem
"Talkin' 2 Myself"	Eminem
"What It's Like"	Everlast
"Superman (It's Not Easy)"	Five For Fighting
"Don't Stop"	Fleetwood Mac
"Go Your Own Way" (59)*	Fleetwood Mac
"Touch Of Grey" (60)*	Grateful Dead
"Drive"	Incubus
"I Feel Good" (61)*	James Brown
"I Can See Clearly Now"	Johnny Nash
"Don't Stop Believing" (62)*	Journey
"Free Bird"	Lynyrd Skynyrd
"Fade To Black"	Metallica
"The Cave"	Mumford & Sons
"If Today Was Your Last Day"	Nickelback
"Home"	Phillip Phillips
"We Will Rock You/We Are The Champions"	Queen

"Dynamite"	Taio Cruz
"Ooh Child" (63)* **	The Five Stairsteps
"I'll Take You There"	The Staple Singers
"Right Now"	Van Halen

* These songs also help. The lyrics speak for themselves. And "Don't Stop Believin'" always makes me smile b/c I am a small-town girl, and Eminem is from Detroit. Find joy where you can! Ha-ha!

** Change the lyric of "We'll walk" to "We'll roll." Ha-ha!

Appreciation/Love

| "Praise You" | Fatboy Slim |

Funny/Feel Good

"Paradise"	Coldplay
"That's All"	Genesis
"Life's Been Good"	Joe Walsh
"Legs"	ZZ Top

Comforting/Love

"Dream On"	Aerosmith
"Jessica"	The Allman Brothers Band
"(Don't Fear) The Reaper"	Blue Oyster Cult
"Layla"	Derek and the Dominos
"You're Never Over"	Eminem
"Sweet Child O' Mine"	Guns N' Roses
"Mercenary Territory"	Little Feat
"Freebird"	Lynyrd Skynyrd
"Every Breath You Take"	Sting, The Police
"She Talks To Angels"	The Black Crowes
"Miss You"	The Rolling Stones

Thank you for taking the time to read my words. I truly hope that they will help you get through any tough times, look ahead to better times, reach those better times and.....

ENJOY

ALL

TIMES!

About the Author

At the 2011 Miss Wheelchair Indiana Pageant
I did not win, but it was a great experience.
The audience loved my jokes!

You already know everything!

Ha–ha–ha!

My Closing Vase

"What a long, strange trip it's been"(64)

Applies to my life's journey.

I cannot wait for what is still to come.

I want to help as many as I can.

I hope you are one of them.

Please have fun in life and smile often!

References

1) The Staple Singers. "I'll Take You There." <u>Be Altitude: Respect Yourself</u>. Stax, 1972. Radio.

2) Reeve, Christopher. Democratic National Convention Speech. 26 Aug. 1996. <http://en.wikiquote.org/wiki/Christopher_Reeve.html>. Retrieved 23 Aug. 2011.

3) Jefferson, Thomas. <http://thinkexist.com/quotes/thomas_jefferson.html>. Retrieved 12 Aug. 2011.

4) Gogh, Vincent van. <http://en.wikiquote.org/wiki/Vincent_van_Gogh>. Retrieved 14 Aug. 2010.

5) Lombardi, Vince. <http://www.vincelombardi.com/quotes.html>. Retrieved 14 Aug. 2010.

6) Lombardi, Vince. <http://www.vincelombardi.com/quotes.html>. Retrieved 14 Aug. 2010.

7) Centers For Pain Relief. 2012. <http://www.centersforpainrelief.com/treatments>. Retrieved 23 Aug. 2012.

8) "Adventures of Handi Man." In Living Color. Greg Fields, Les Firestein, Keenan Ivory Wayans, Pam Veasey Damon Wayans. Fox. 1990–1994.

9) ZZ Top. "Legs." <u>Eliminator</u>. Warner Bros, 1983. CD.

10) Genesis. "That's All." <u>Genesis</u>. Atlantic, Virgin, Vertigo, 1983. CD.

11) Reeve, Christopher. <http://en.wikiquote.org/wiki/Christopher_Reeve>. Retrieved 16 Aug. 2010.

12) Eagles. "Already Gone." On The Border. Asylum, 1974. CD.

13) Marley, Bob. "Trenchtown Rock." Rastaman Vibration Disc 2: Live Edition. Tuff Gong/Island, 1976. CD.

14) NIckelback. "If Today Was Your Last Day." Dark Horse. Roadrunner, 2008. CD.

15) Cruz, Taio. "Dynamite." Rockstarr. Island, 2010. CD.

16) Queen. "We Will Rock You/We Are The Champions." Single, EMI, 1977. CD.

17) Fleetwood Mac. "Don't Stop." Rumours. Warner Bros., 1976. CD.

18) Five for Fighting. "Superman (It's Not Easy)." American Town. EMI, 2000. CD.

19) Alabama. "I'm In A Hurry." Single. RCA Records, 1992. CD.

20) Boston. "Peace Of Mind." Boston. Epic, 1976. CD.

21) Incubus. "Drive." Make Yourself. Epic/Immortal, 2000. CD.

22) Mumford & Sons. "The Cave." Sigh No More. Island, 2010. CD.

23) Bob Marley & The Wailers. "No Woman, No Cry." Natty Dread. 1974. CD.

24) Bob Marley & The Wailers. "Three Little Birds." Exodus. Tuff Gong, 1980. CD.

25) Bob McFerrin. "Don't Worry, Be Happy." Simple Pleasures. 1998. CD.

26) Eminem. "Cinderella Man." Recovery. Aftermath/Shady, 2010. CD.

27) Eminem. "Talkin' 2 Myself." Recovery. Aftermath/Shady, 2010. CD.

28) Van Halen. "Right Now." <u>For Unlawful Carnal Knowledge</u>. Warner Bros.,

1992. CD.

29) Aerosmith. "Dream On." <u>Aerosmith</u>. Columbia, 1973. CD.

30) Dave Matthews Band. "Best of What's Around." <u>Under the Table and</u>

<u>Dreaming</u>. RCA, 1994. CD.

31) Dave Matthews Band. "Everyday." <u>Everyday</u>. RCA, 2001. CD.

32) Metallica. "Fade To Black." <u>Ride The Lightning</u>. Megaforce, Elektra, 1984.

CD.

33) Fatboy Slim. "Praise You." <u>You've Come a Long Way, Baby</u>. Skint, 1998. CD.

34) Eminem. "You're Never Over." <u>Recovery</u>. Aftermath/Shady, 2010. CD.

35) The Rolling Stones. "Miss You." <u>Some Girls</u>. Rolling Stones, 1978. CD.

36) The Allman Brothers Band. "Jessica." <u>An Evening With The Allman Brothers</u>

<u>Band: 2nd Set</u>. Epic, 1995. CD.

37) Derek and the Dominos. "Layla." <u>Layla and Other Assorted Love Songs</u>.

Atco/RSO/Polydor, 1970. CD.

38) Lynyrd Skynyrd. "Freebird." <u>(pronounced 'lĕh-'nérd 'skin-'nérd)</u>. MCA,

1973. CD.

39) The Black Crowes. "She Talks To Angels." <u>Shake Your Money Maker</u>. Def

America, 1990. CD.

40) Little Feat. "Mercenary Territory." <u>The Last Album</u>. Warner Bros., 1975. CD.

41) Blue Oyster Cult. "(Don't Fear) The Reaper." <u>Agents Of Fortune</u>. Columbia,

1976. CD.

42) <u>Saturday Night Live: More Cowbell</u>. Dir. .2000. Television.

43) Miss Me But Let Me Go. <http://www.funeral-poems.net/funeral-poem/
miss-me-let-me-go>. Retrieved 14 Aug 2010.

44) Nash, Johnny. "I Can See Clearly Now." Single. Epic, 1972. CD.

45) Eminem. "Not Afraid." <u>Recovery</u>. Aftermath/Shady, 2010. CD.

46) Lombardi, Vince. <http://www.brainyquote.com/quotes/quotes/v/
vincelomba121925.html. Retrieved 14 Aug 2010.

47) Jobs, Steve. 2005 Stanford Commencement Address. <http://
news.stanford.edu/news/2005/june15/jobs-061505.html>. Retrieved 14
Aug 2010.

48) Mother Teresa. Life poem. <http://www.turnbacktogod.com/mother-
teresa-poem-life/>. Retrieved 14 Aug 2010.

50) <Http://www.inspire.com>.

51) Everlast. "What It's Like." <u>Whitey Ford Sings the Blues</u>. Tommy Boy Records,
1998. CD.

52) Guns N'Roses. "Sweet Child O' Mine." <u>Appetite For Destruction</u>. Geffen,
1998. CD.

53) Sting, The Police. "Every Breath You Take." <u>Synchronicity</u>. A&M, 1983. CD,

54) Lombardi, Vince. <http://www.vincelombardi.com/quotes.html>. Retrieved
10 Aug 2010.

55) Coldplay. "Paradise." <u>Mylo Xyloto</u>. Parlophone, 2011. CD.

56) Joe Walsh. "Life's Been Good." <u>But Seriously, Folks.....</u>. Single. Asylum, 1978.

   CD.

57) Phillip Phillips. "Home." Single. Interscope, 2012. CD.

58) Chumbawumba. "Tubthumping." <u>Tubthumper</u>. Universal Records, 1997. CD.

59) Fleetwood Mac. "Go Your Own Way." Single. Warner Bros., 1976. CD.

60) Grateful Dead. "Touch Of Grey." <u>In The Dark</u>. Arista, 1987. CD.

61) James Brown. "I Got You (I Feel Good)." <u>I Got You (I Feel Good)</u>. King, 1965.

   CD.

63) Journey. "Don't Stop Believin'." Single. Buddah Records, 1970. CD.

63) The Five Stairsteps. "Ooh Child." Single. Buddah Records, 1970. CD.

64) Grateful Dead. "Truckin'." <u>American Beauty</u>. Warner Bros., 1970. CD.

Dreams Continued:

As I said, my main goal with this book is to achieve my life dream of helping people. I also mentioned my dreams of modeling and remodeling (Ha-ha). I would also be helping others with both of those. Along with these I do have a couple dreams, or wishes, with not so many beneficiaries:

1) I would love to take my mom on a long trip somewhere.

2) Go to Lambeau and see a Packers' game. Of course I would sit in the front row of the end zone so I could hug the player when he does the leap, and get a game ball (that I would then have autographed by the players after the game). Maybe I could even give the pre-game speech! Ha-ha!!!!

3) I would love to meet The Rolling Stones and hear them play "Miss You."

4) The same with Metallica and "Fade to Black."

5) The same with Dave Matthews Band and "Everyday."